HOW TO DRAW A CUTE ANIMALS FOR KIDS: VOL. 2

LEARN TO DRAW CUTE ANIMALS, FUNNY FOOD AND OBJECTS WITH A STEP BY STEP GUIDE

THIS BOOK TEACHES YOU
HOW TO DRAW IN A SIMPLE AND FUNNY WAY.

DISCOVER THE 36 DRAWINGS OF ANIMALS,
MARINE CREATURES, OBJECTS AND FOOD.

HOW DOES IT WORK:
YOU ONLY NEED A PENCIL AND A SHEET.
FOLLOW
THE VARIOUS STEPS THAT THE FIGURES SHOW YOU.

BECOME A TRUE ARTIST.

LET'S FUN

WRITE YOUR NAME

LET'S START
LEARNING
TO DRAW ANIMALS

ELEPHANT

FIRST STEPS

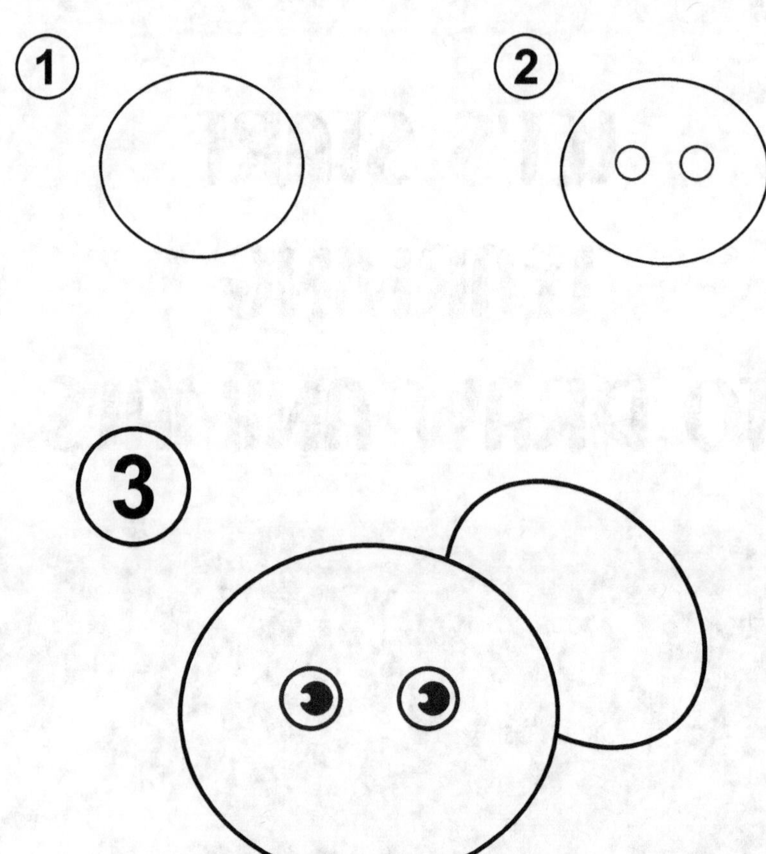

ELEPHANT

SECOND STEP

4

5

6

ELEPHANT

FINISHED

TRY TO DRAW IT HERE

ELEPHANT

KANGAROO

FIRST STEPS

KANGAROO

SECOND STEP

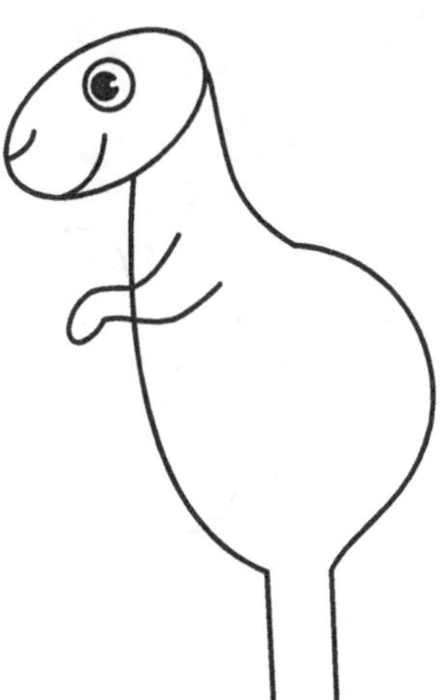

6

7

8

9

KANGAROO

FINISHED

TRY TO DRAW IT HERE

KANGAROO

HEN

FIRST STEPS

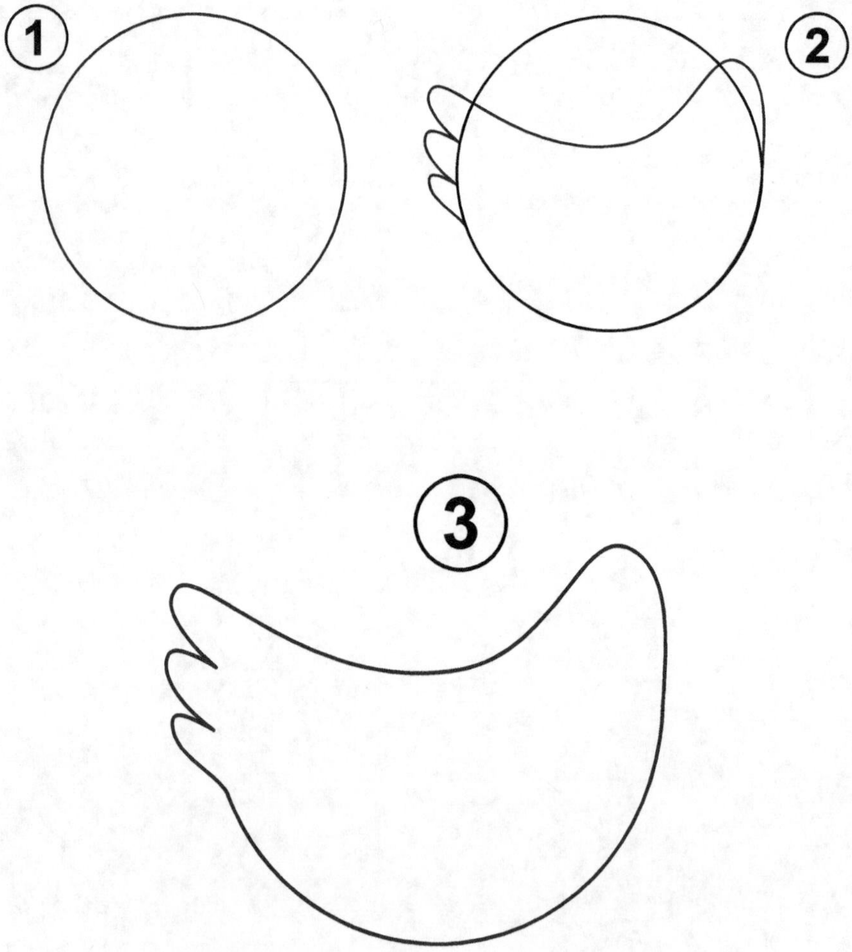

① ② ③

HEN

SECOND STEP

FINISHED

7

8

9

TRY TO DRAW IT HERE

HEN

OWL

FIRST STEPS

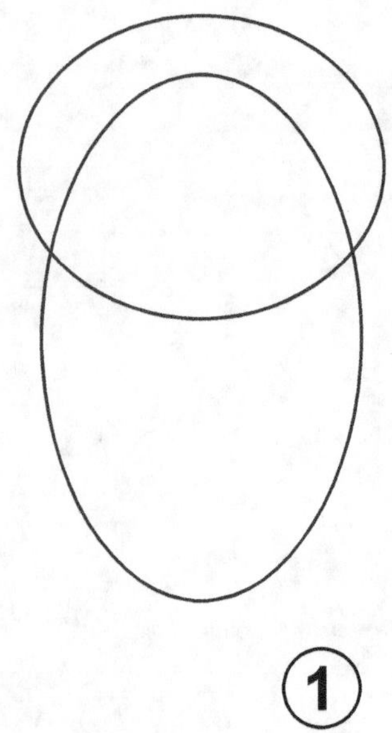

1

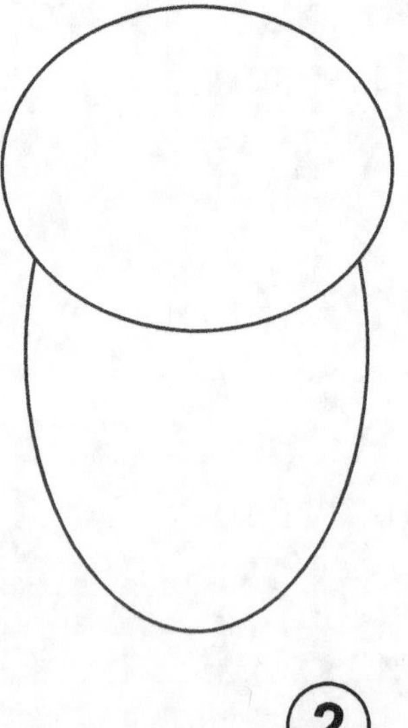

2

SECOND STEP

③

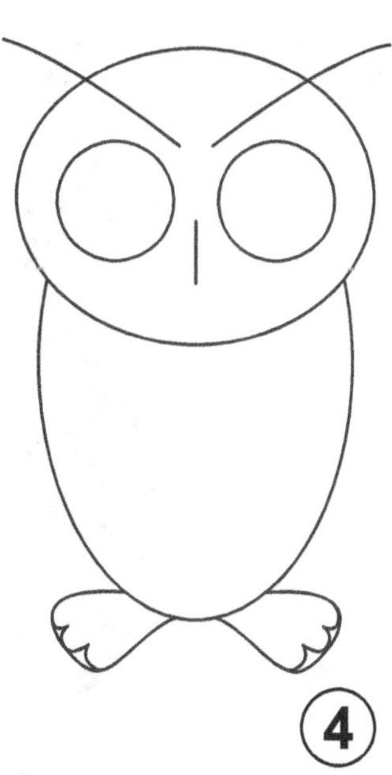

④

FINISHED

TRY TO DRAW IT HERE

OWL

FIRST STEPS

① ②

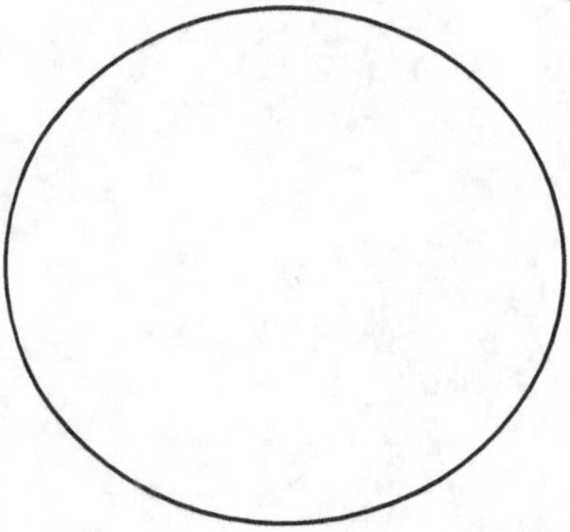

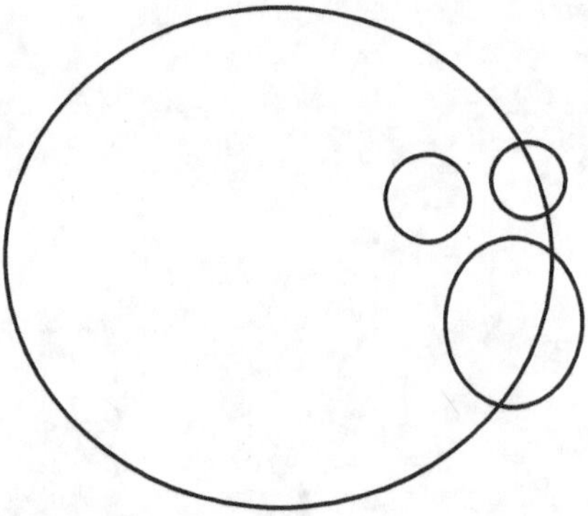

③

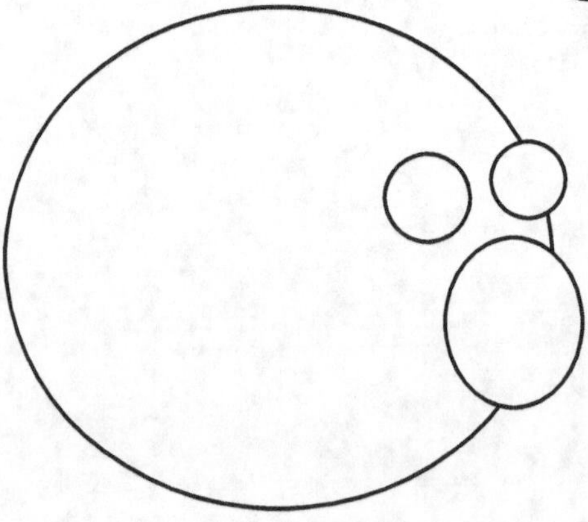

PIG

SECOND STEP

FINISHED

TRY TO DRAW IT HERE

PIG

FIRST STEPS

1

2

3

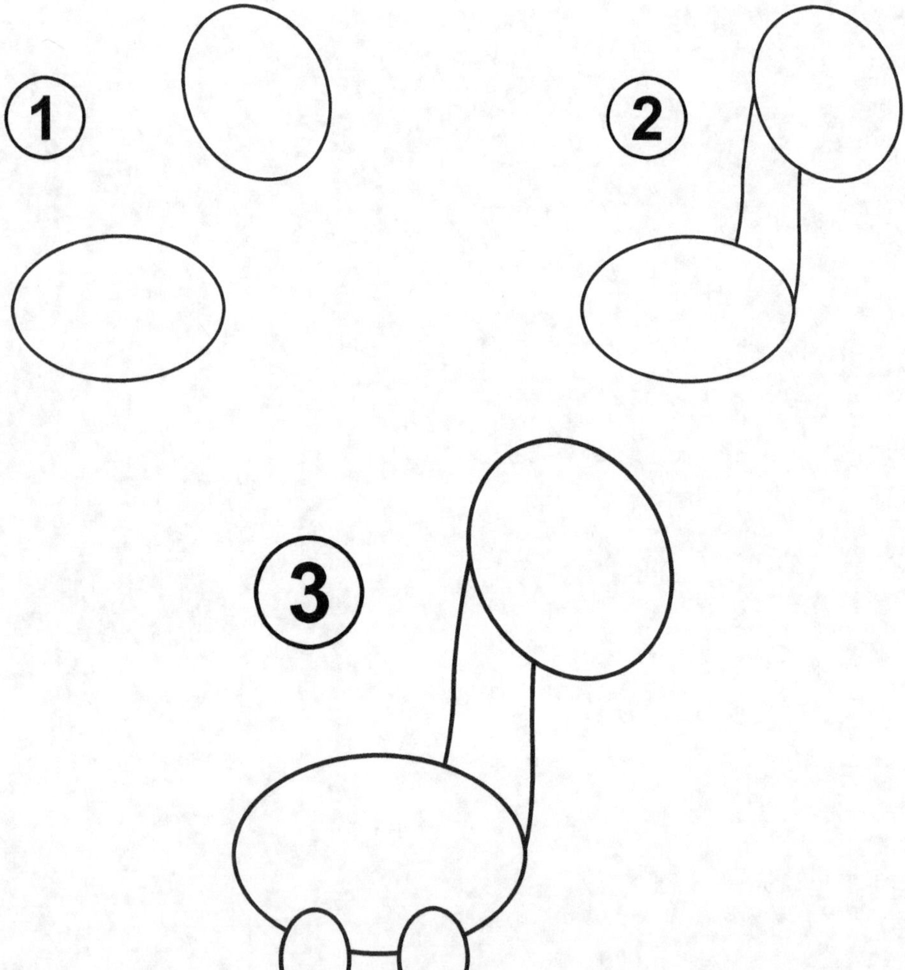

SECOND STEP

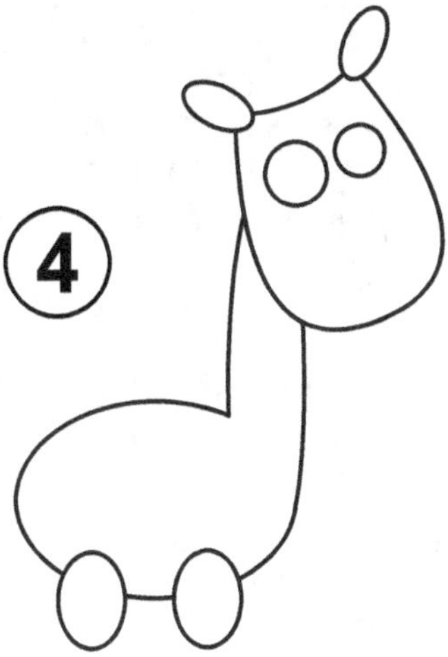

FINISHED

TRY TO DRAW IT HERE

GIRAFFE

KOALA

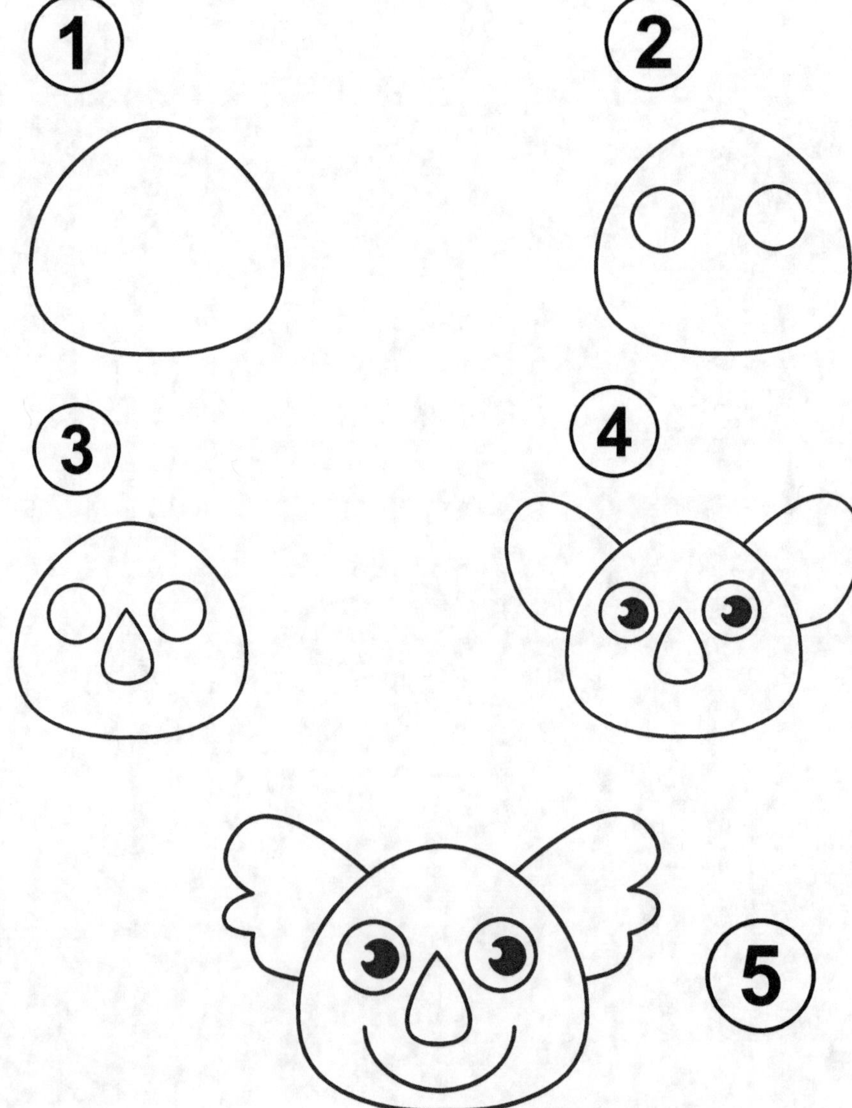

KOALA

SECOND STEP

FINISHED

10

11

12

13

TRY TO DRAW IT HERE

KOALA

SHEEP

FIRST STEPS

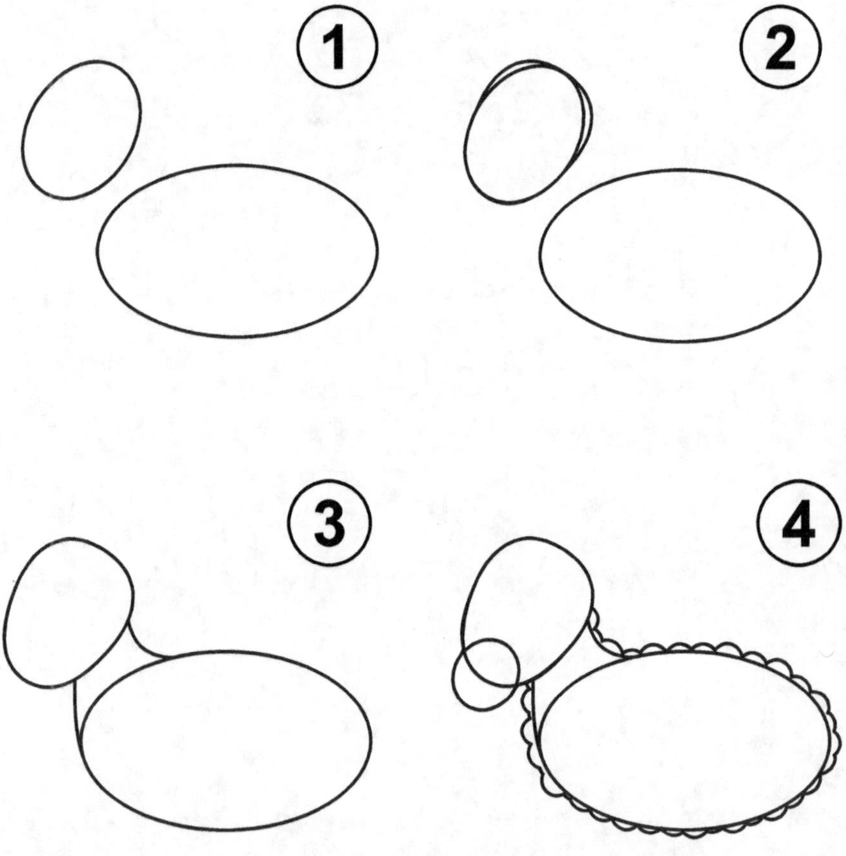

SHEEP

SECOND STEP

SHEEP

FINISHED

TRY TO DRAW IT HERE

SHEEP

FIRST STEPS

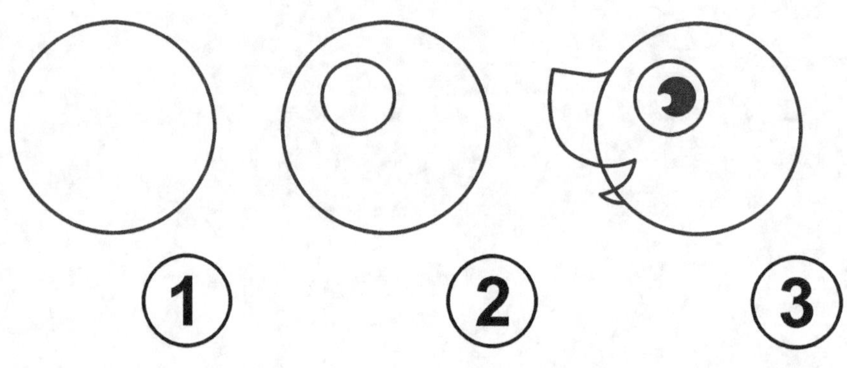

SKUNK

SECOND STEP

7

8

9

10

FINISHED

TRY TO DRAW IT HERE

SKUNK

BUTTERFLY

FIRST STEPS

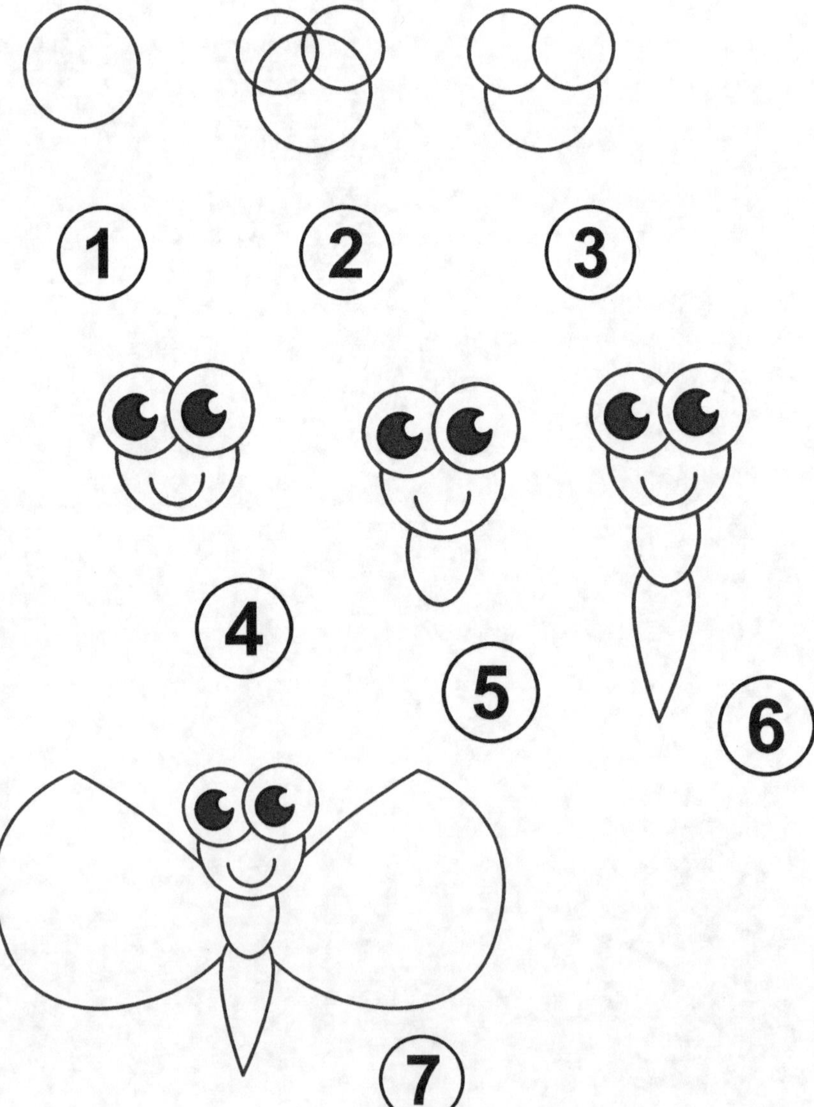

SECOND STEP

FINISHED

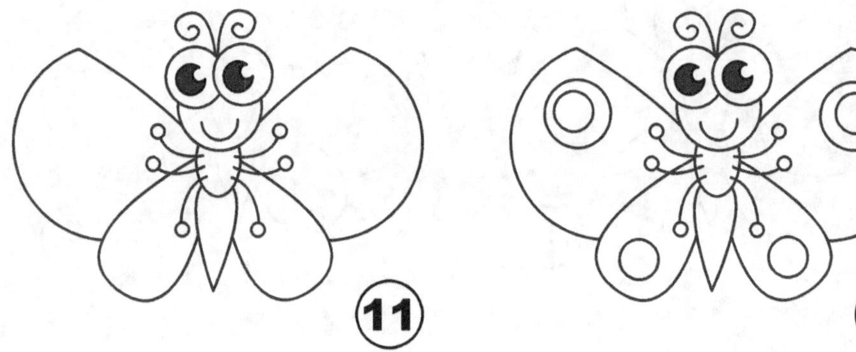

TRY TO DRAW IT HERE

BUTTERFLY

WOODPECKER

FIRST STEPS

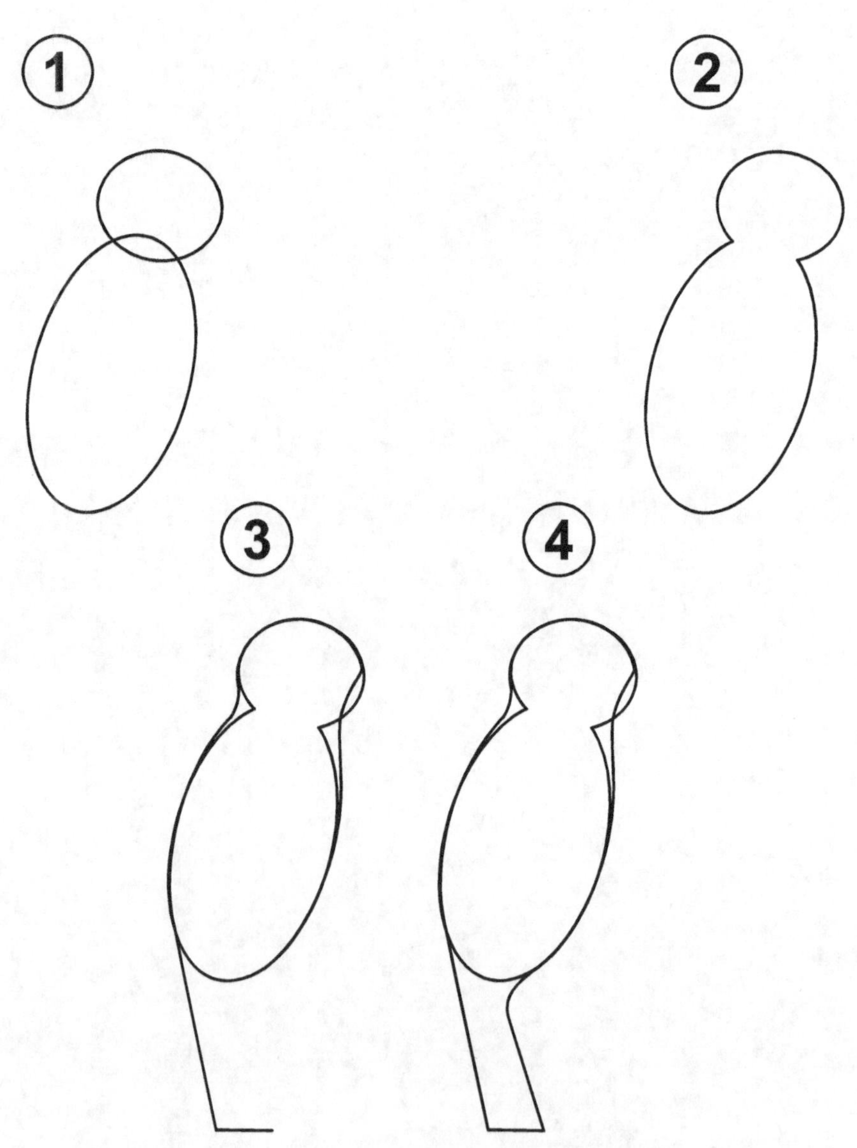

WOODPECKER

SECOND STEP

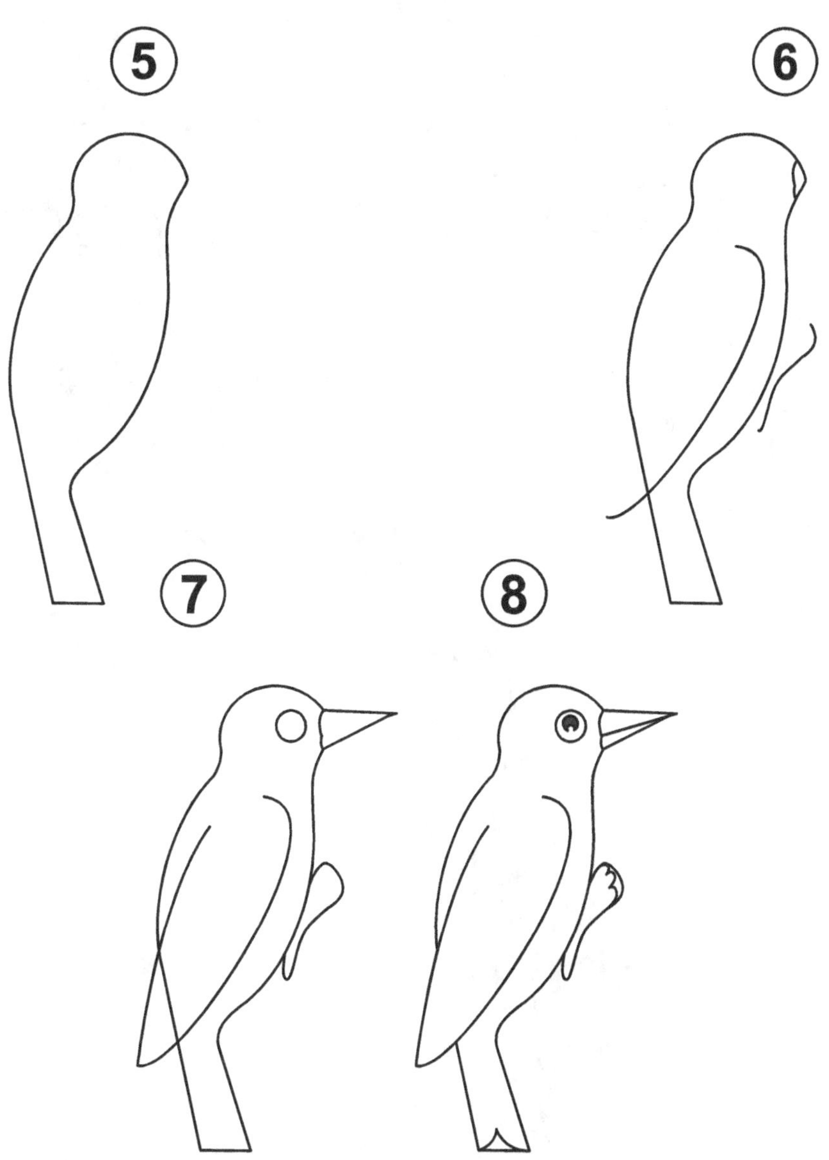

WOODPECKER

FINISHED

⑨

⑩

⑪

TRY TO DRAW IT HERE

WOODPECKER

PARROT

FIRST STEPS

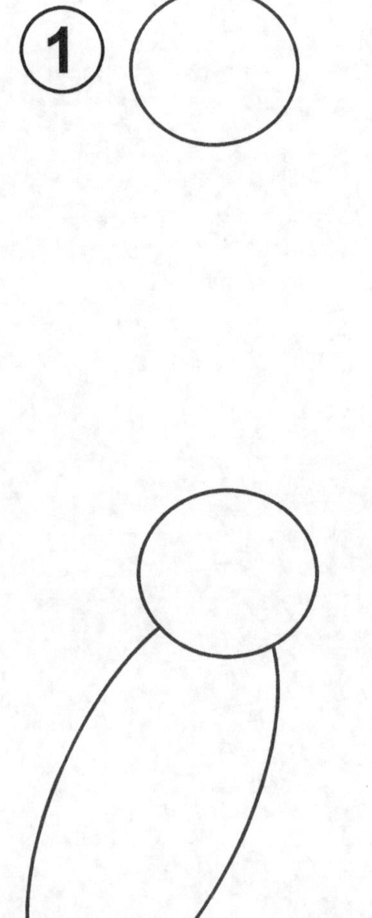

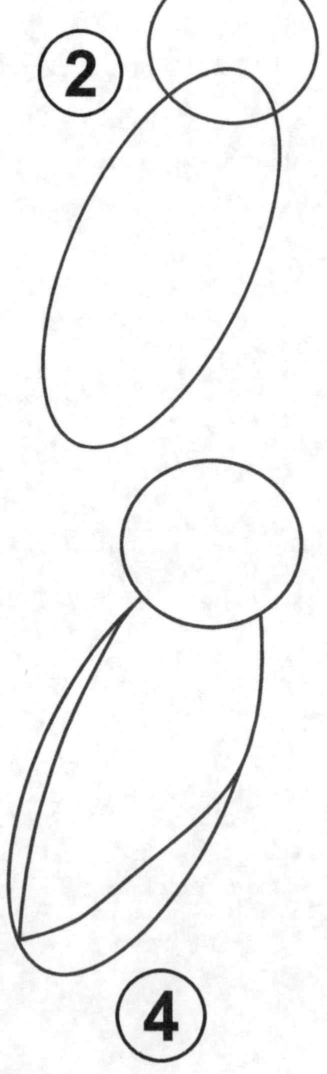

PARROT

SECOND STEP

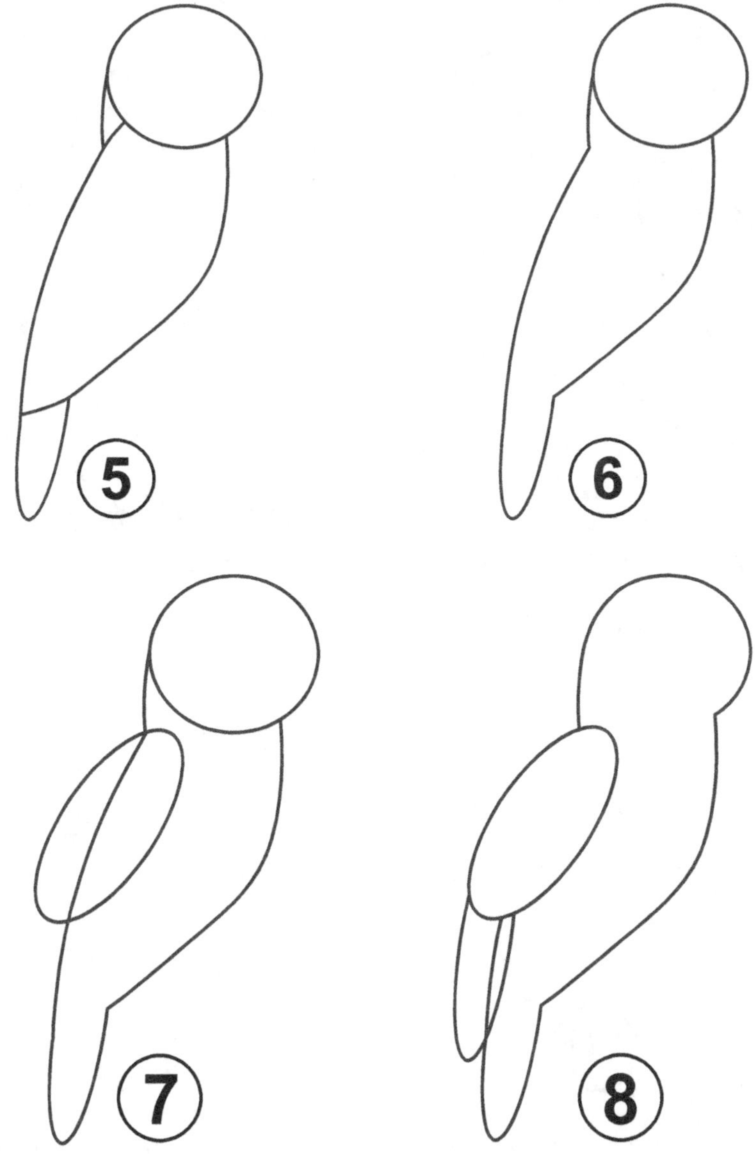

PARROT

THIRD STEP

PARROT

FINISHED

TRY TO DRAW IT HERE

PARROT

LET'S START LEARNING TO DRAW SEA CREATURES

DOLPHIN

FIRST STEPS

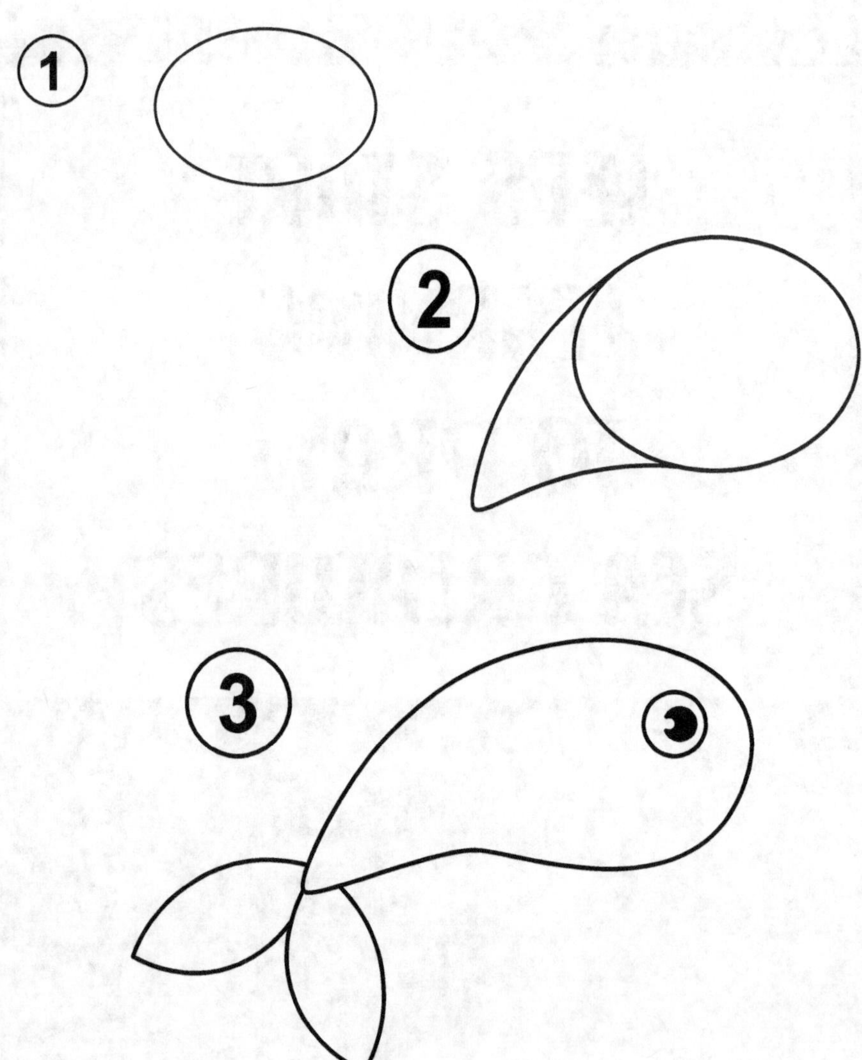

DOLPHIN

SECOND STEP

DOLPHIN

FINISHED

TRY TO DRAW IT HERE

DOLPHIN

GOSLING

FIRST STEPS

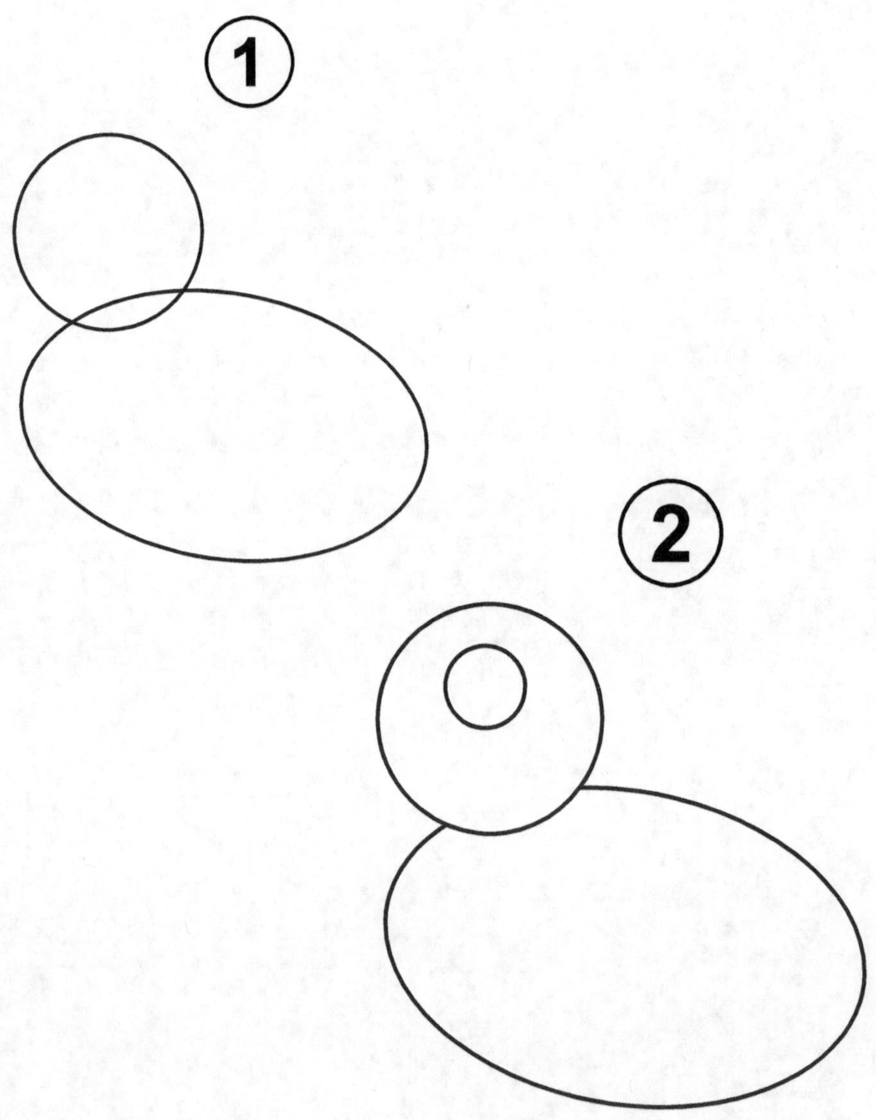

GOSLING

SECOND STEP

GOSLING

FINISHED

5

6

TRY TO DRAW IT HERE

GOSLING

LOBSTER

FIRST STEPS

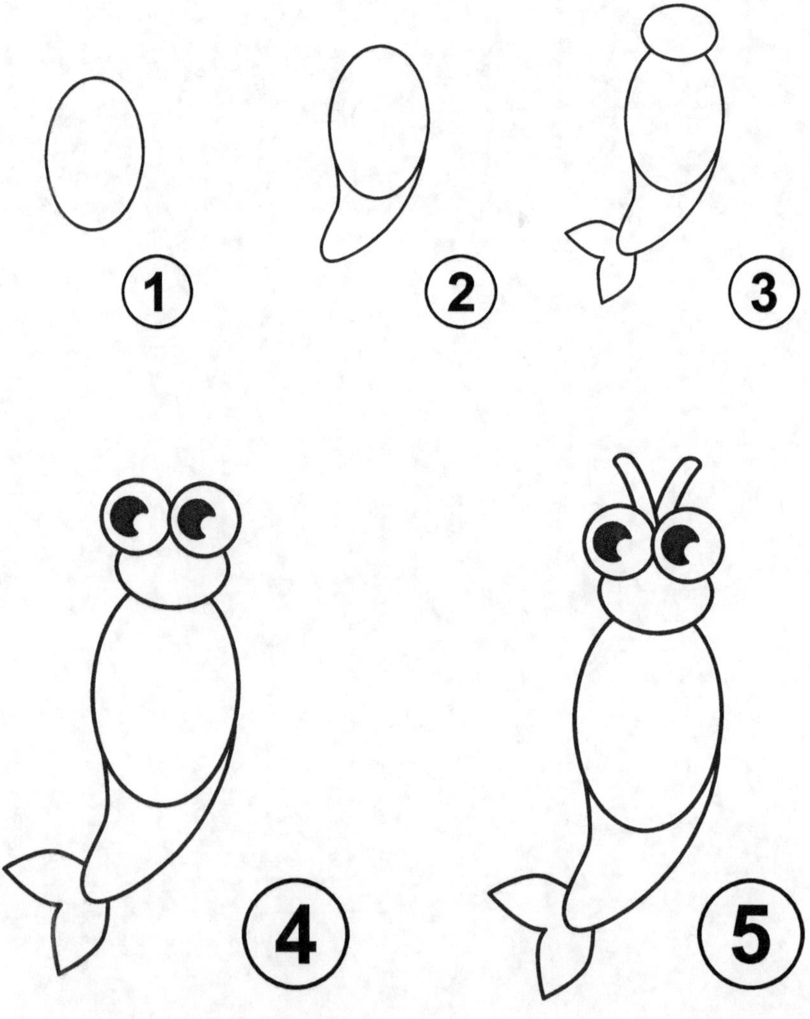

LOBSTER

SECOND STEP

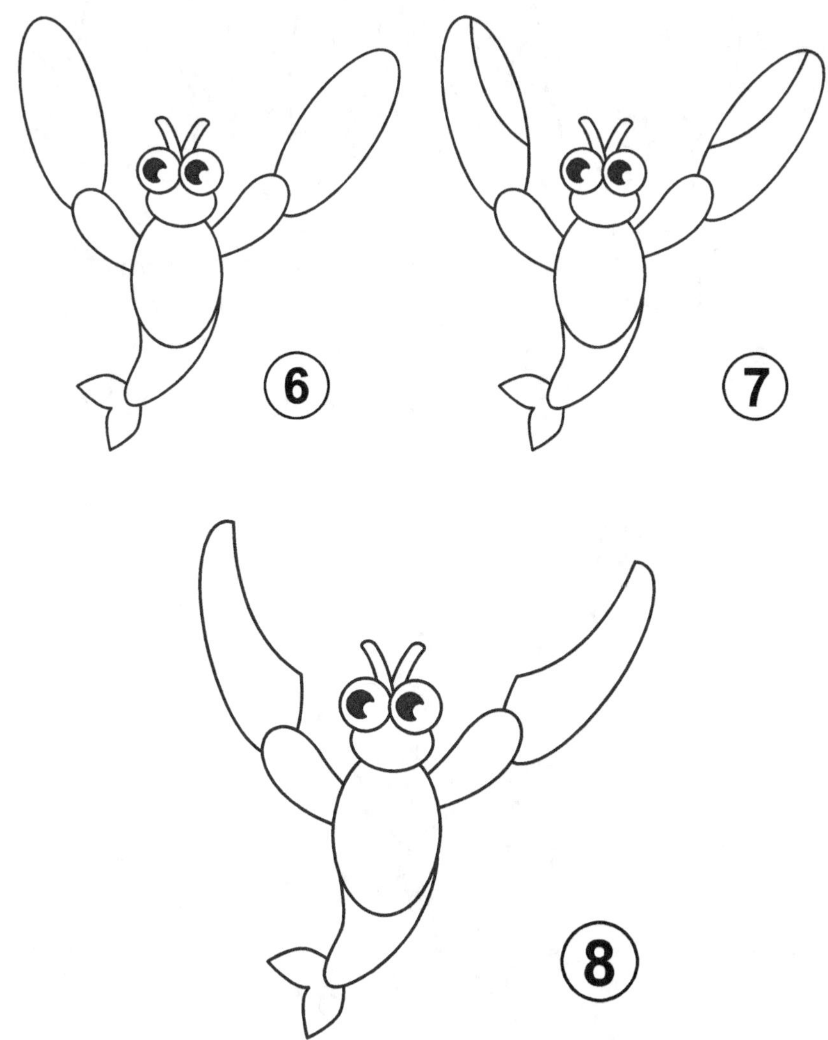

LOBSTER

FINISHED

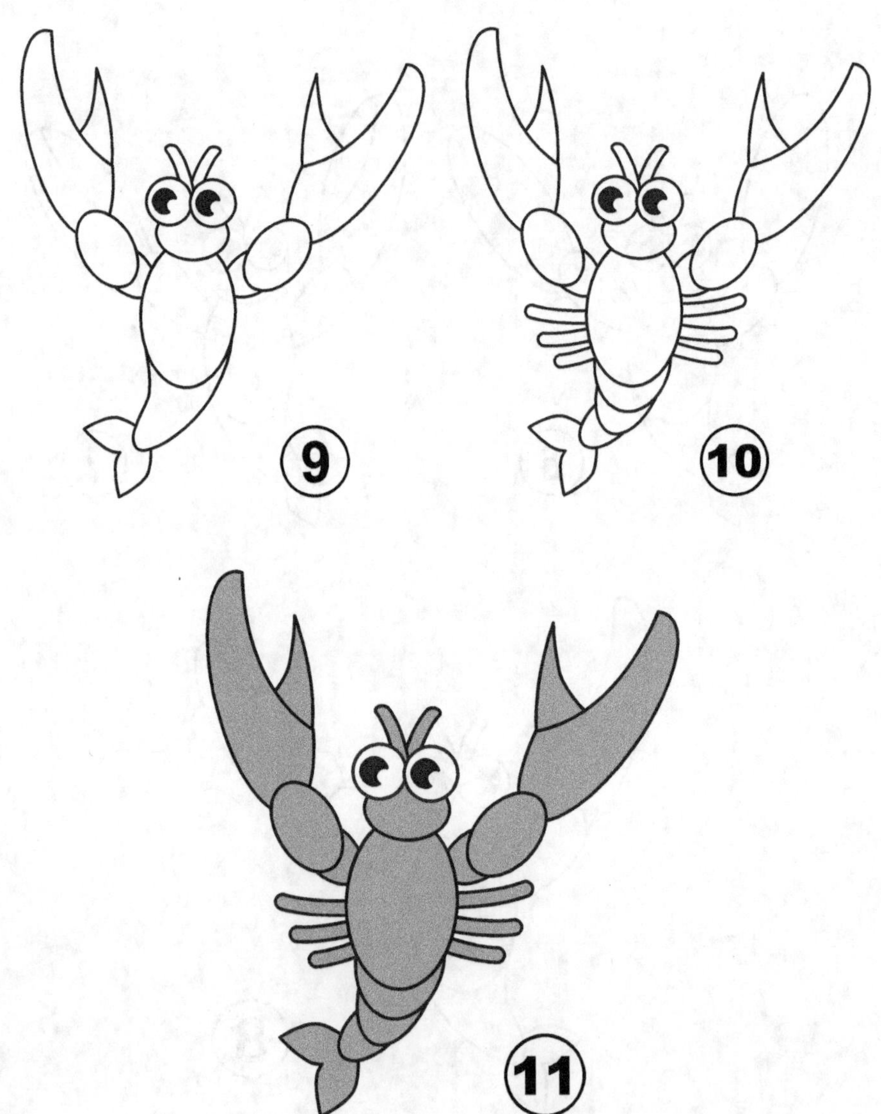

TRY TO DRAW IT HERE

LOBSTER

HERMIT CRAB

FIRST STEPS

HERMIT CRAB

SECOND STEP

HERMIT CRAB

FINISHED

TRY TO DRAW IT HERE

HERMIT CRAB

SEASHELL

FIRST STEPS

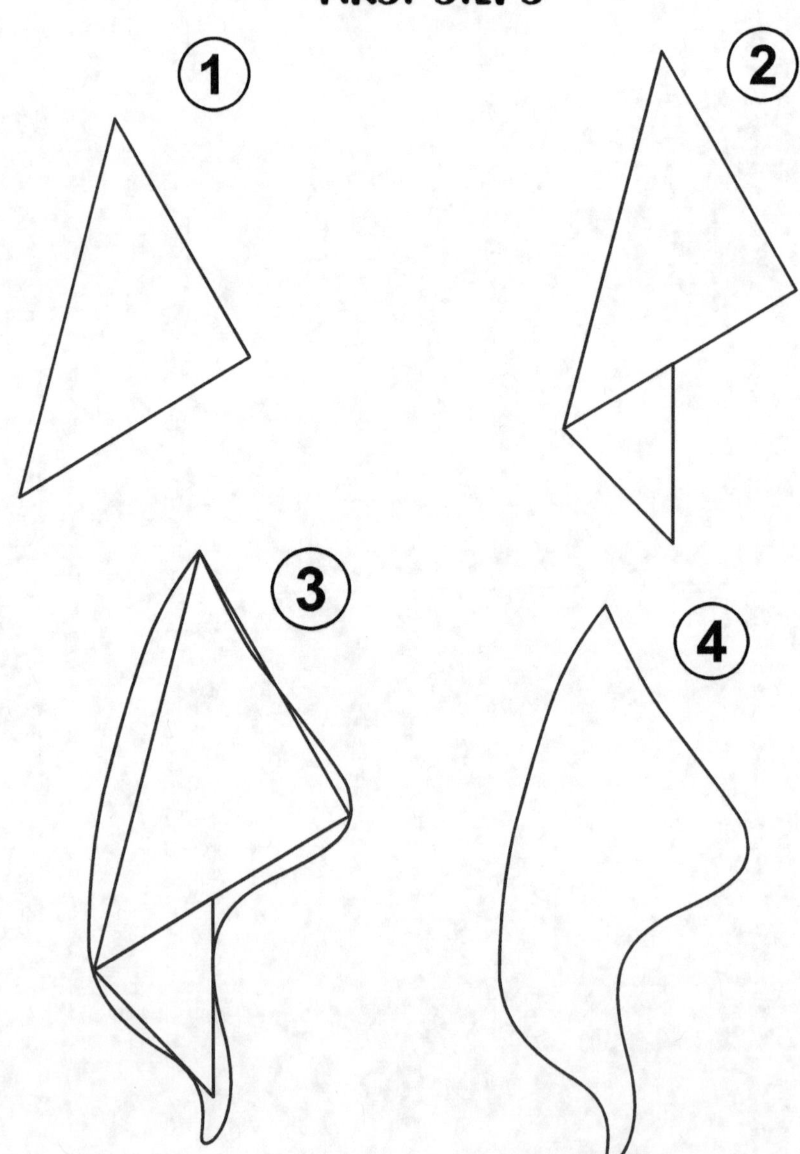

SEASHELL

SECOND STEP

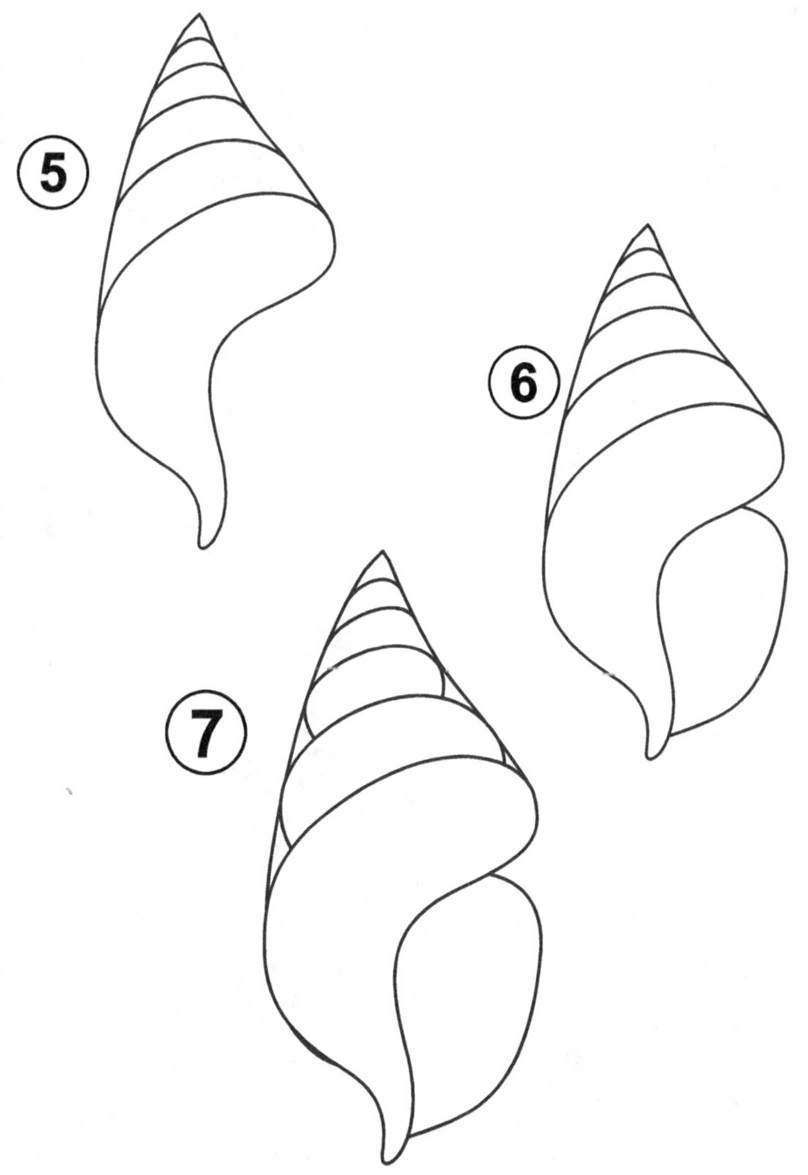

FINISHED

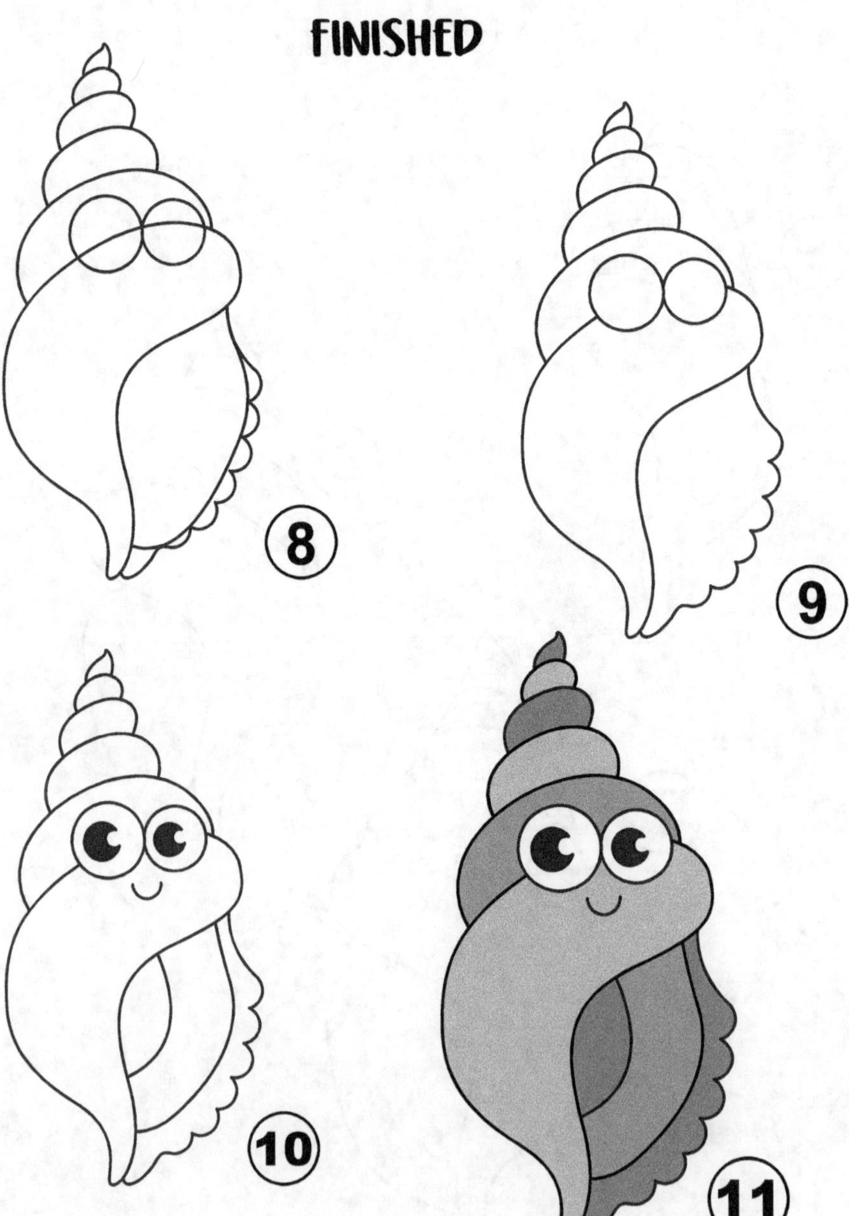

TRY TO DRAW IT HERE

SEASHELL

X-RAY FISH

FIRST STEPS

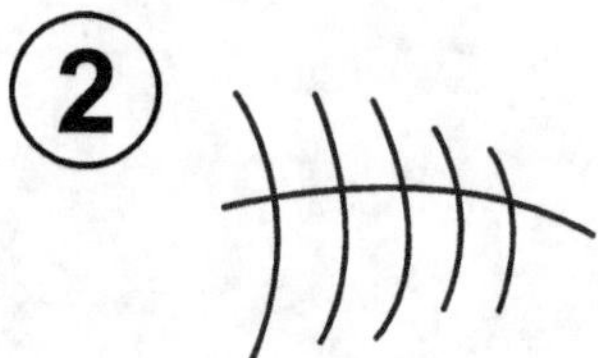

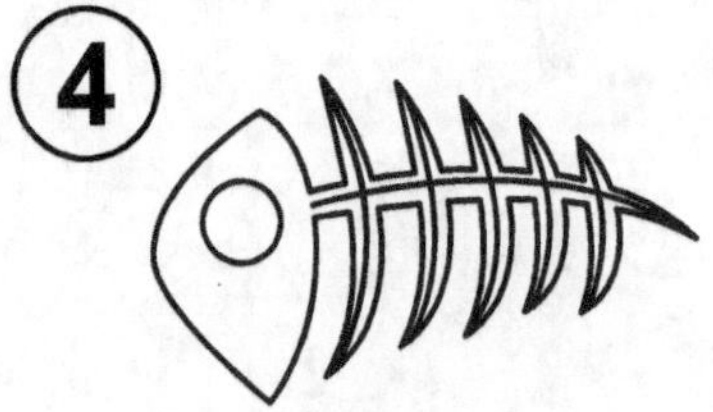

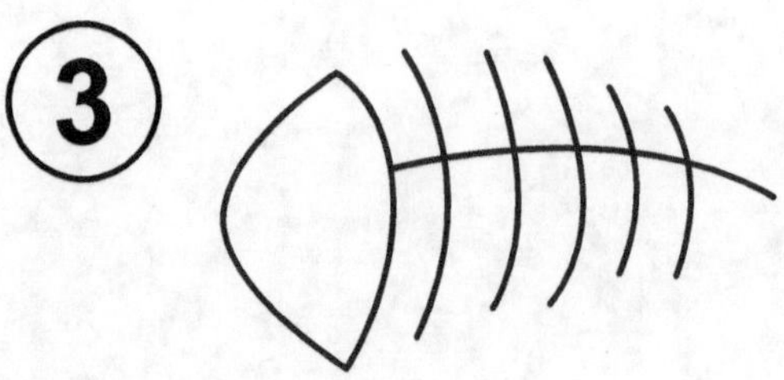

X-RAY FISH

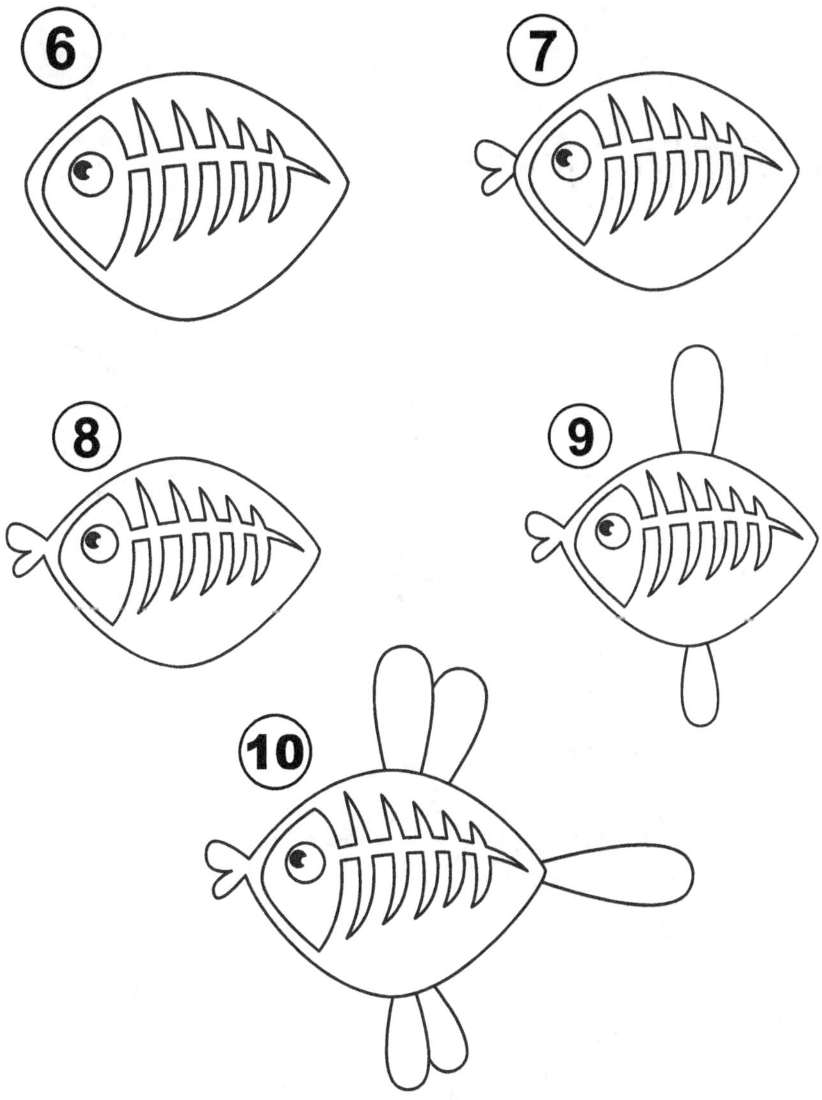

X-RAY FISH

FINISHED

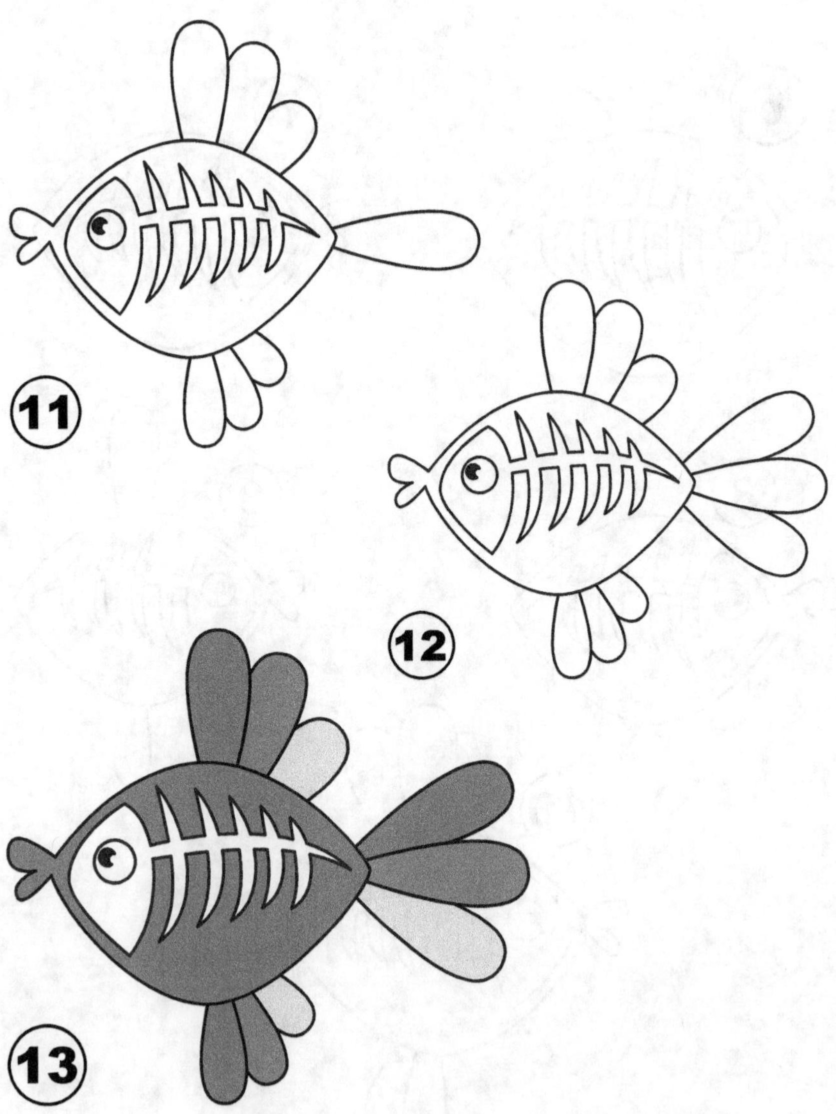

TRY TO DRAW IT HERE

X-RAY FISH

candy
LET'S START
LEARNING
TO DRAW FOOD
Burger
Cake

FIRST STEPS

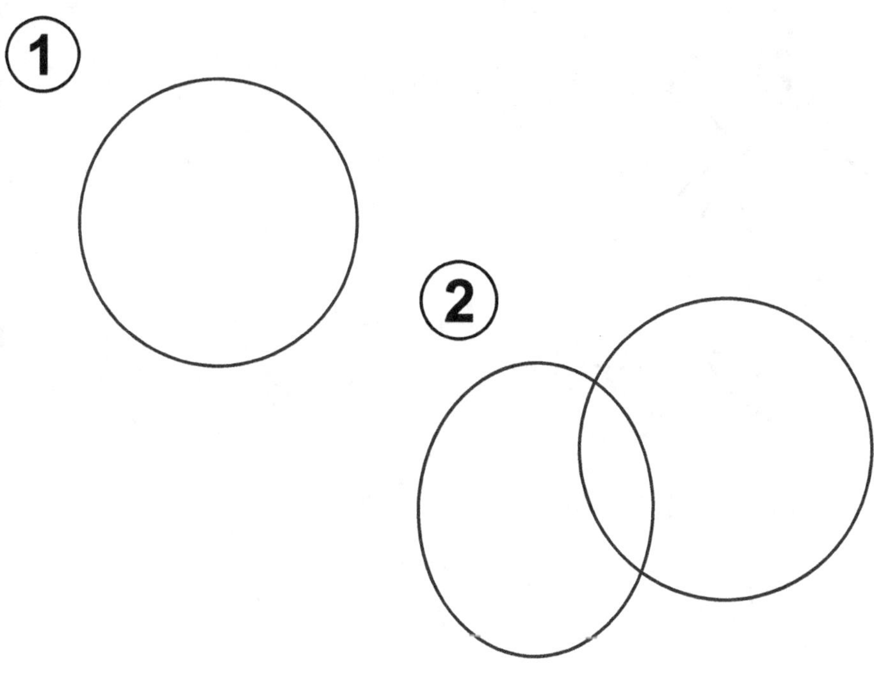

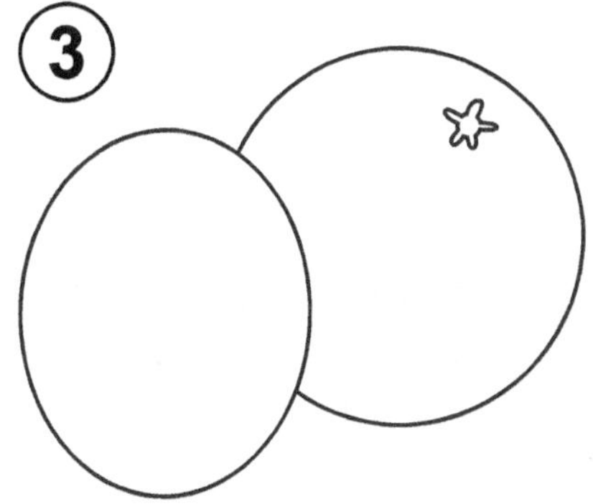

ORANGE

SECOND STEP

4

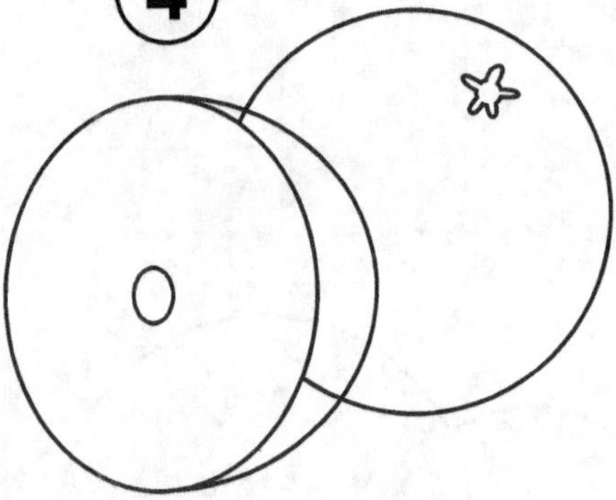

5

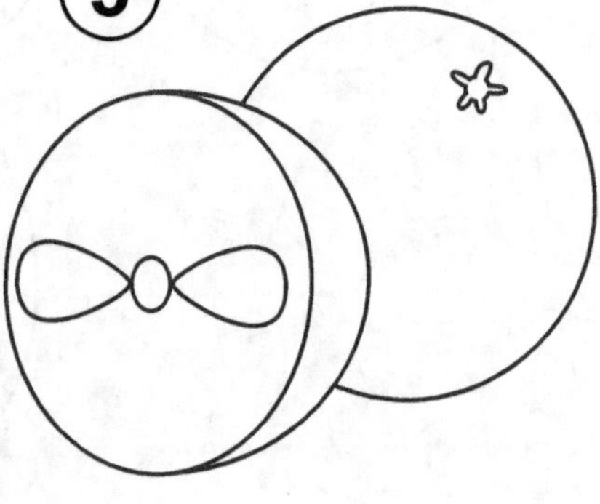

6

ORANGE

FINISHED

7

8

9

TRY TO DRAW IT HERE

ORANGE

BANANA

FIRST STEPS

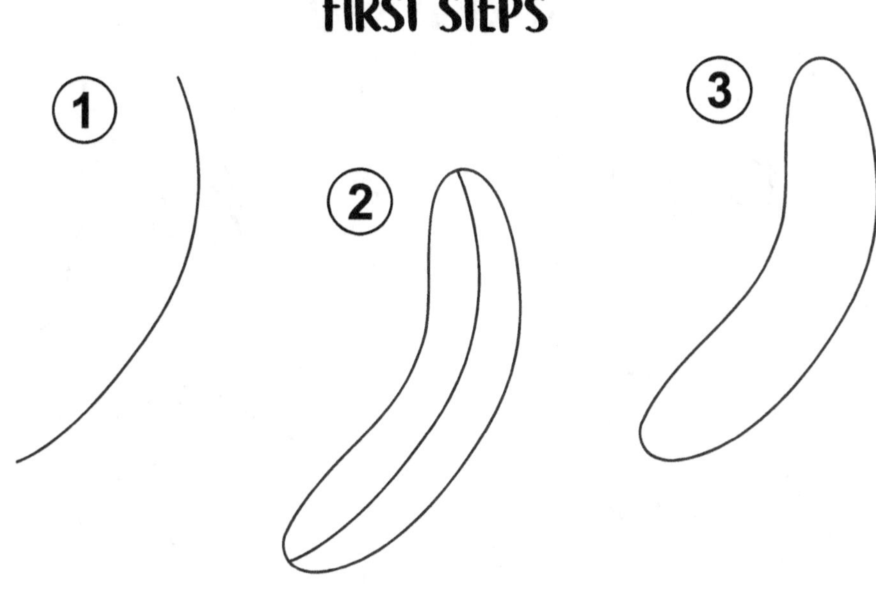

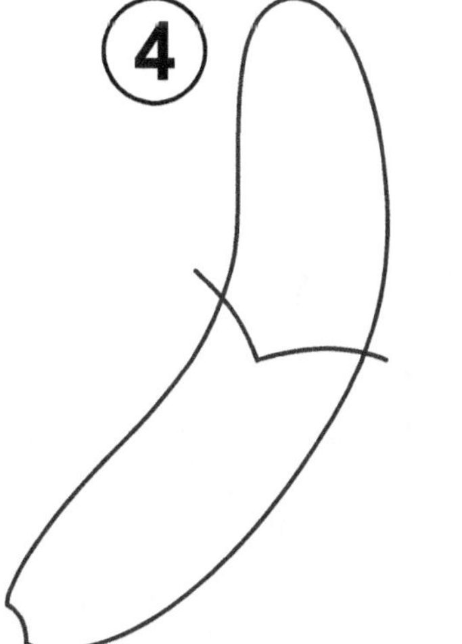

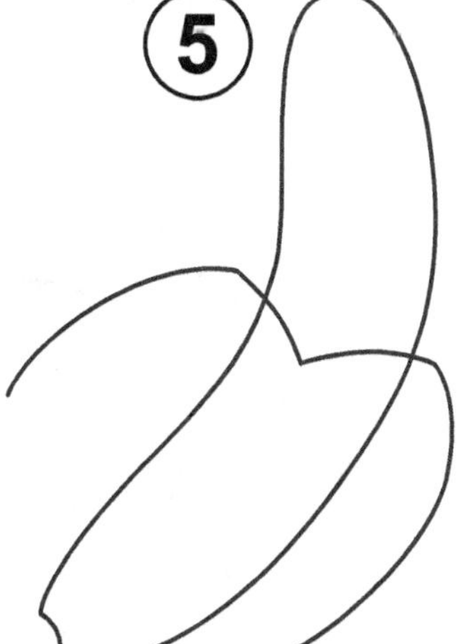

BANANA

SECOND STEP

6

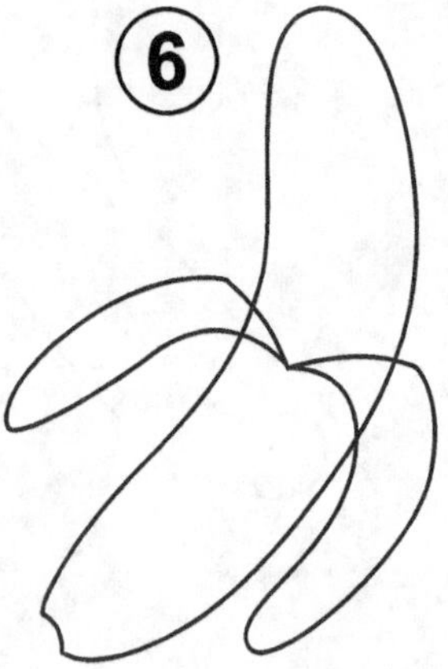

7

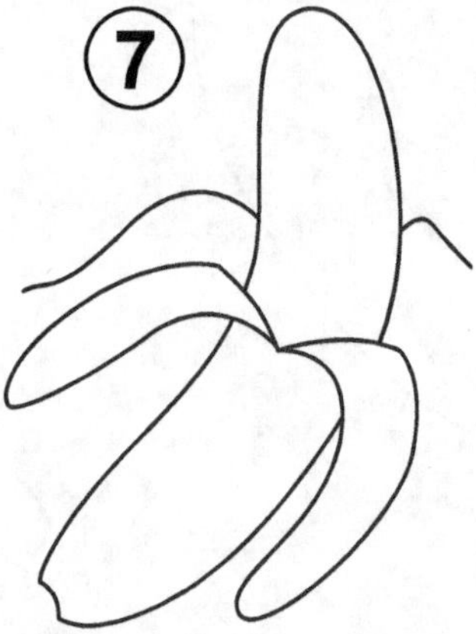

8

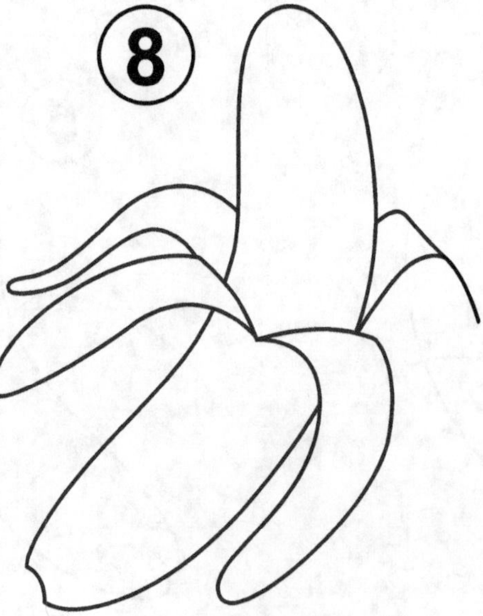

BANANA

FINISHED

⑨

⑩

⑪

TRY TO DRAW IT HERE

BANANA

CHERRY

FIRST STEPS

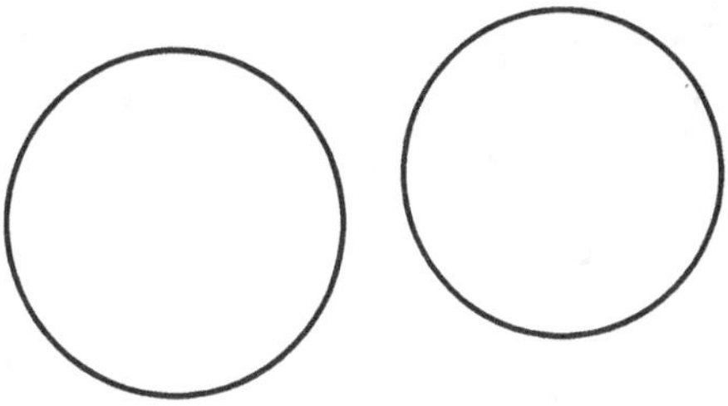

1

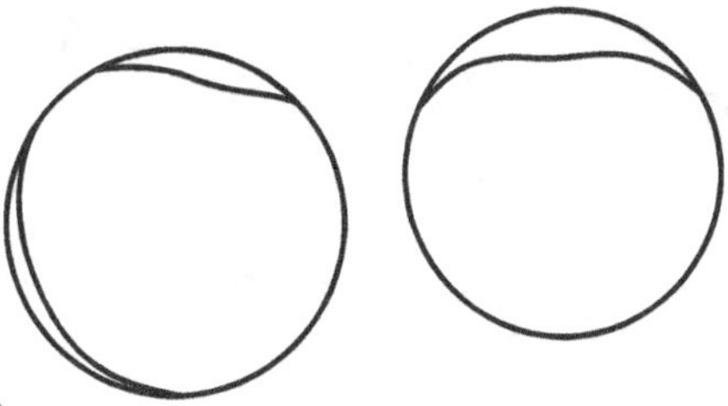

2

3

CHERRY

SECOND STEP

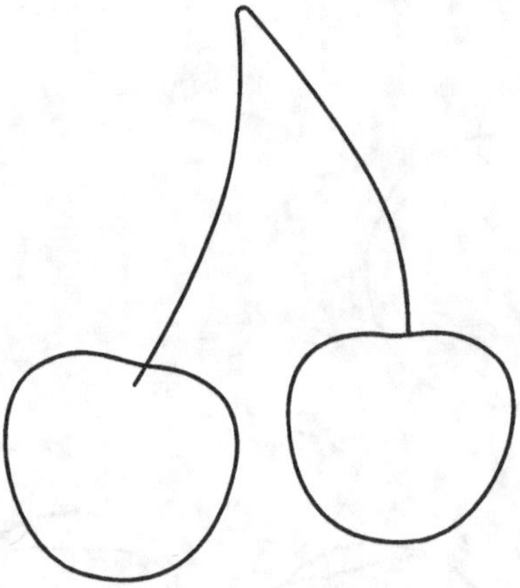

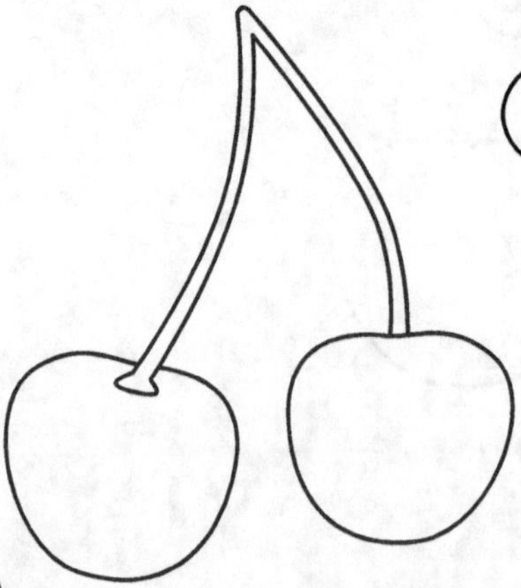

CHERRY

FINISHED

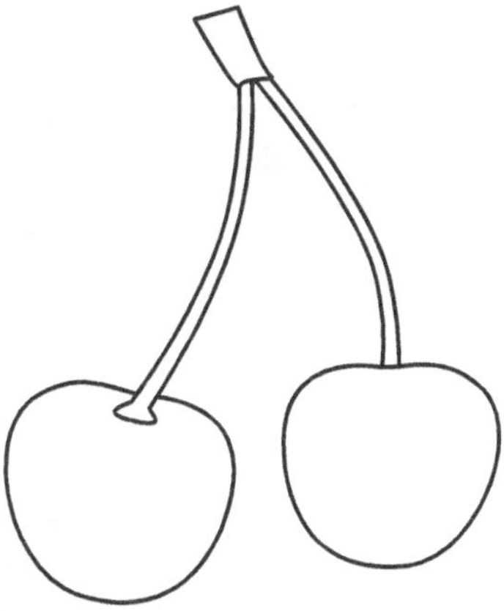

⑦

⑧

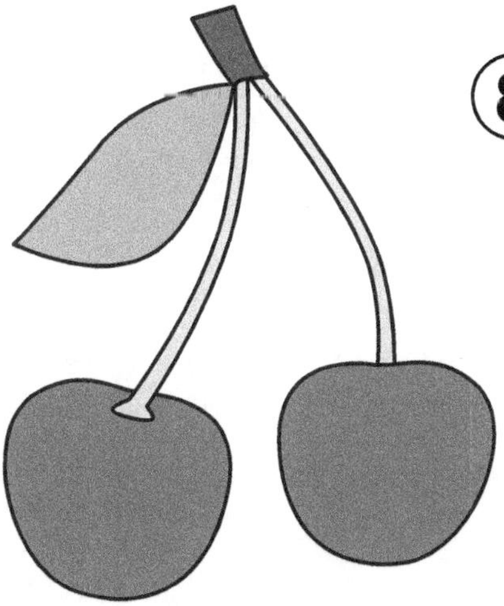

⑨

TRY TO DRAW IT HERE

CHERRY

FIRST STEPS

1

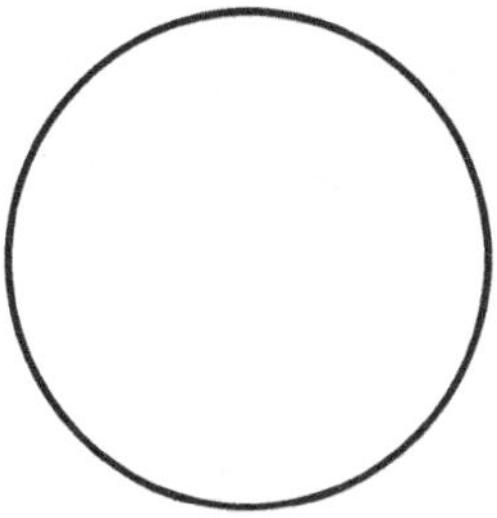

2

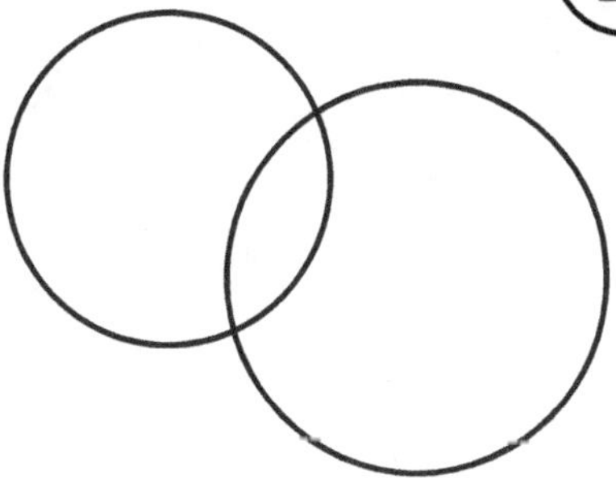

3

SECOND STEP

4

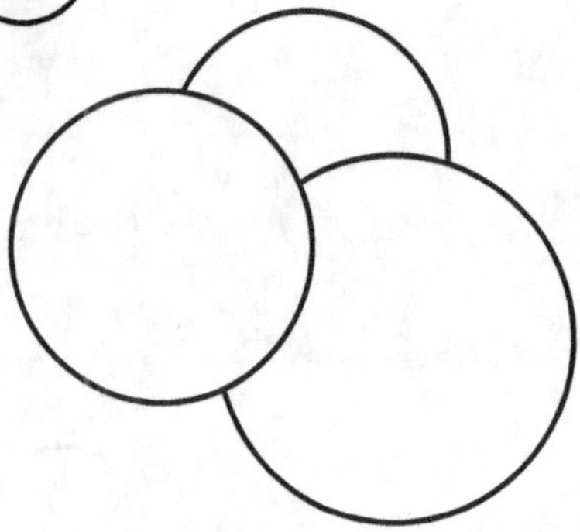

5

6

ICE CREAM
FINISHED

7
8
9

TRY TO DRAW IT HERE

ICE CREAM

ICE CREAM

ONION

FIRST STEPS

①

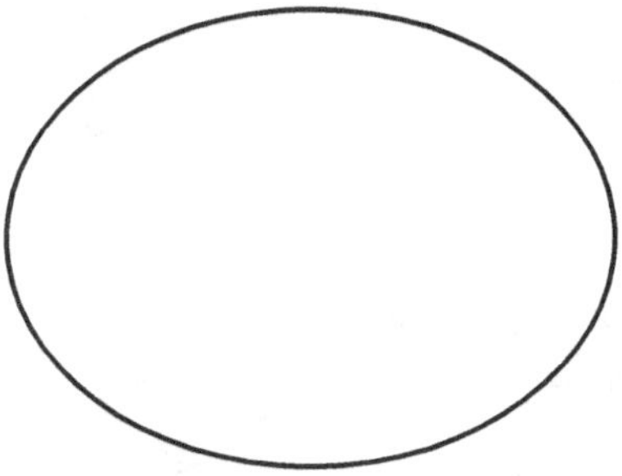

②

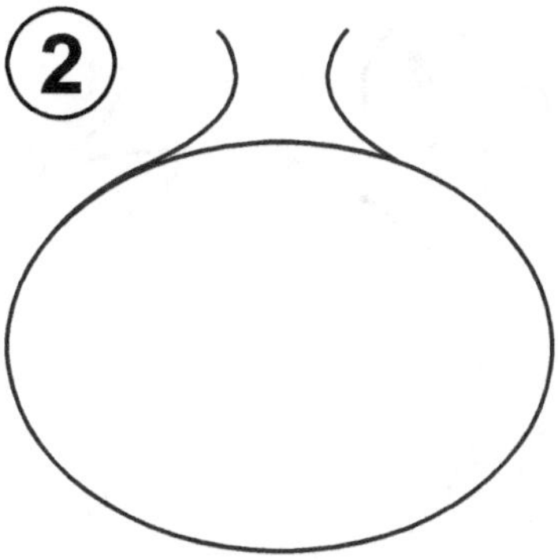

③

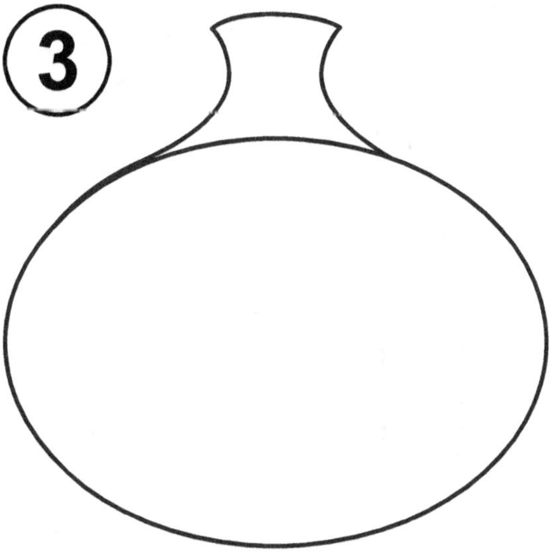

ONION

SECOND STEP

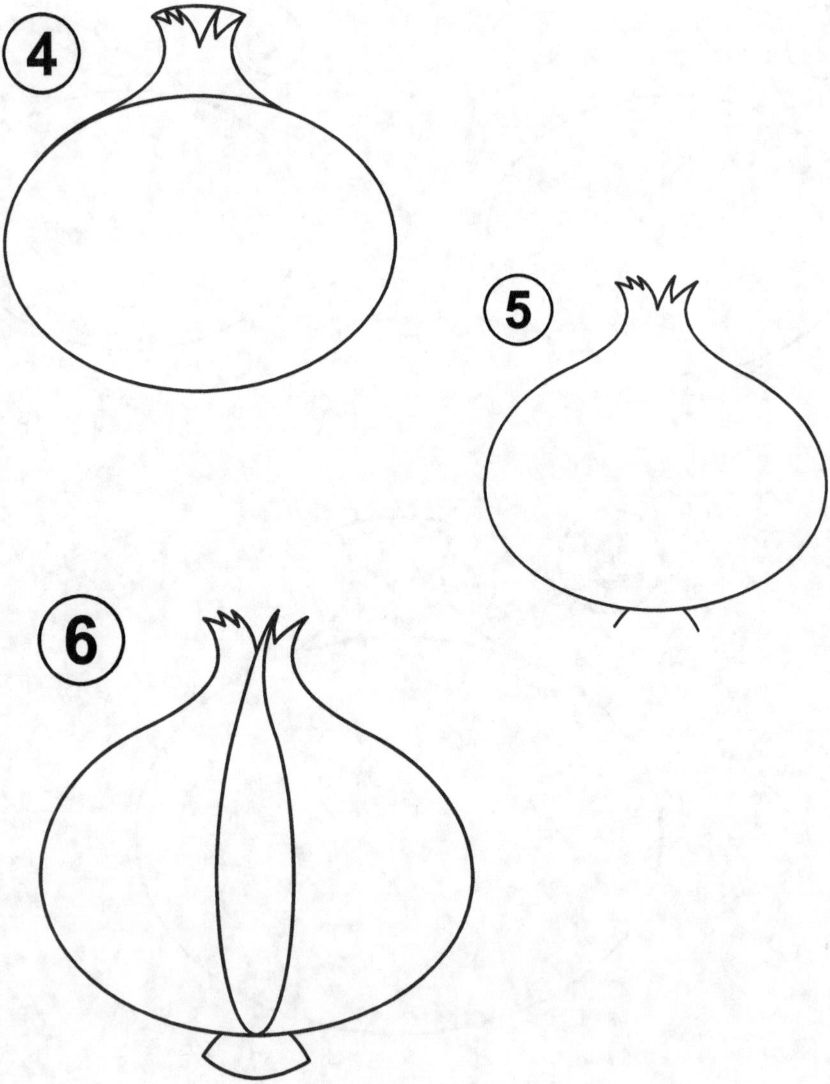

4

5

6

ONION

FINISHED

⑦

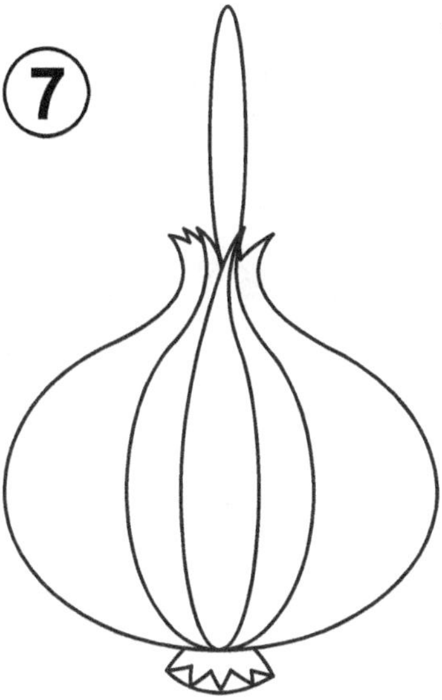

⑧

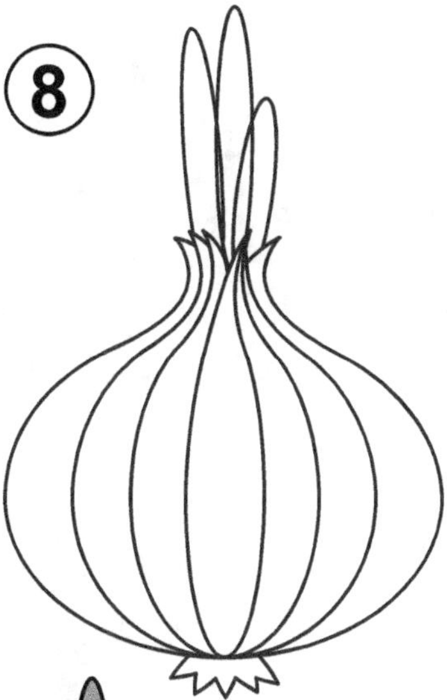

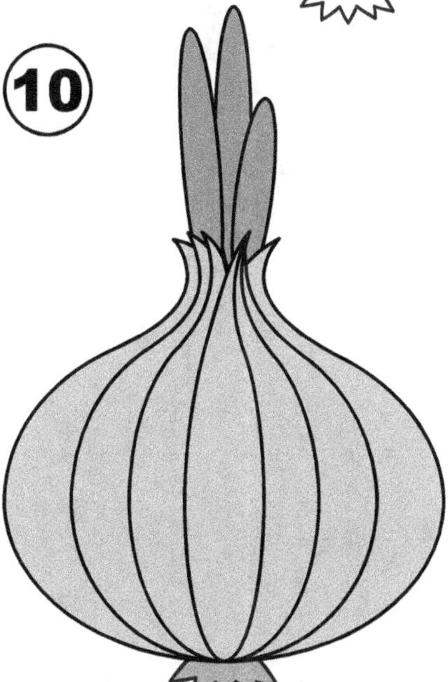

⑨

⑩

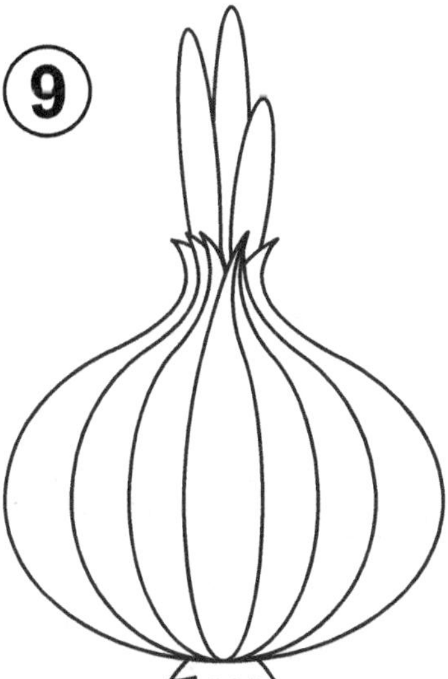

TRY TO DRAW IT HERE

ONION

EASTER EGGS

FIRST STEPS

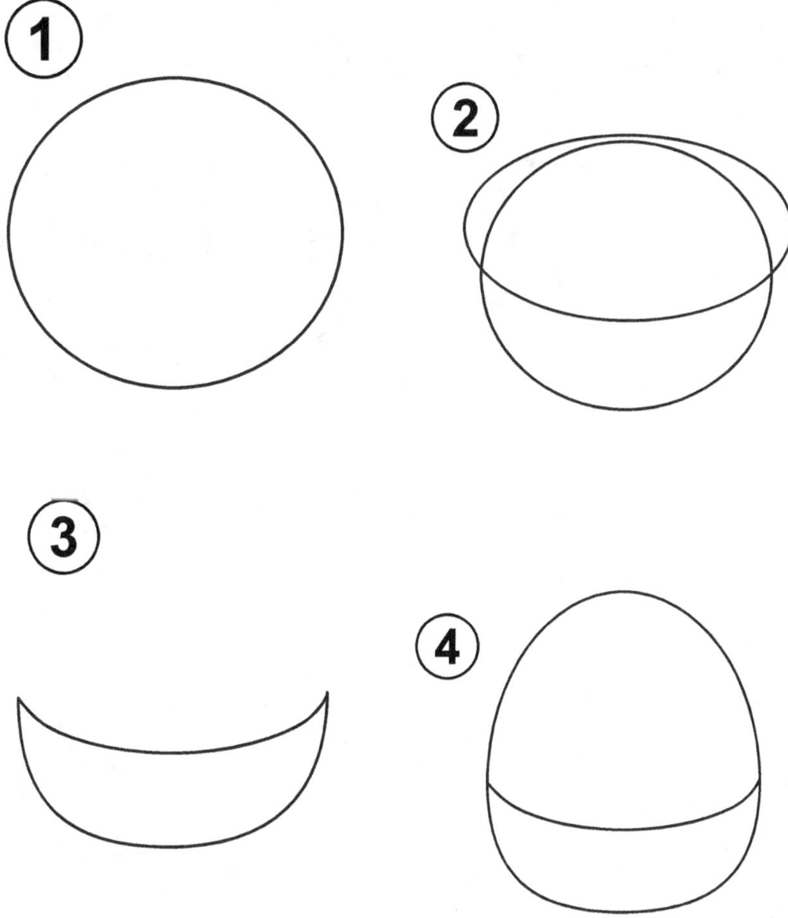

EASTER EGGS

SECOND STEP

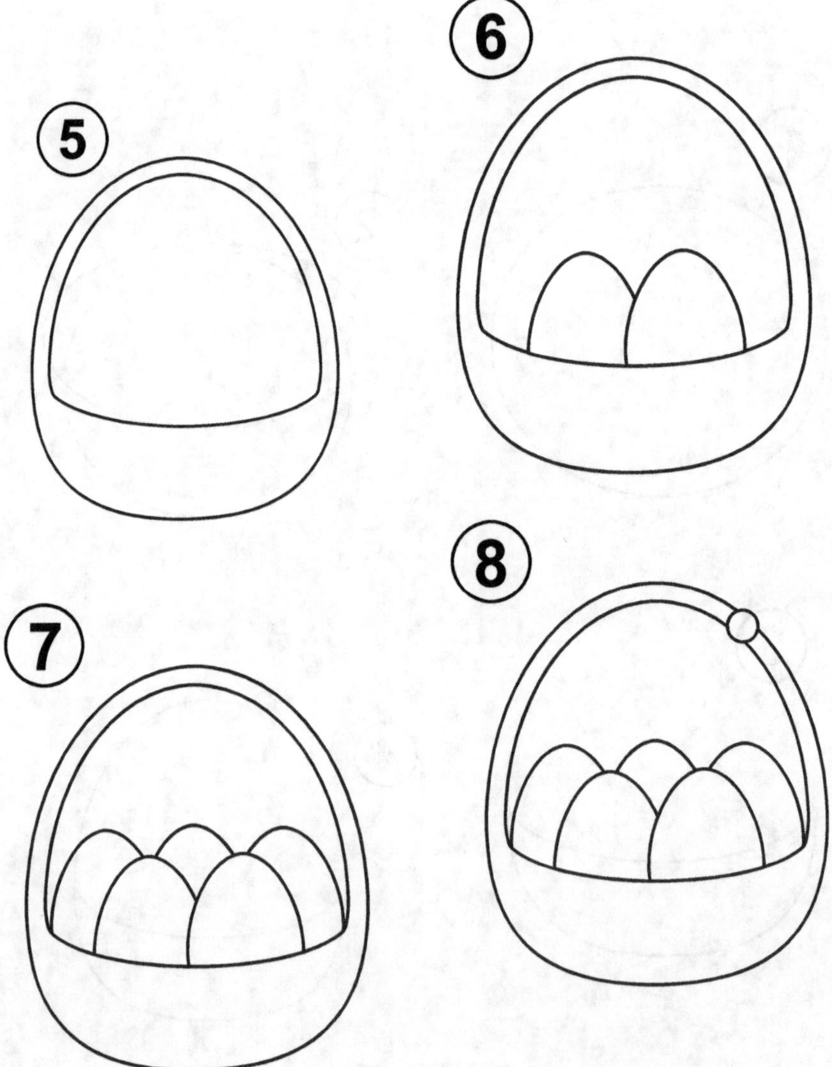

FINISHED

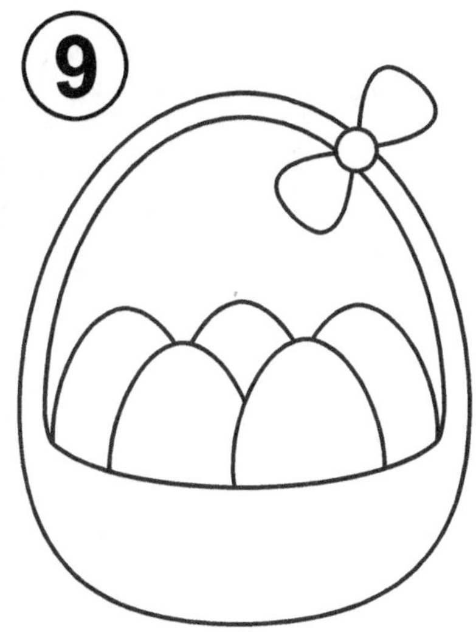

TRY TO DRAW IT HERE

EASTER EGGS

LET'S START LEARNING
TO DRAW OBJECTS

SPORTS BALLS

FIRST STEPS

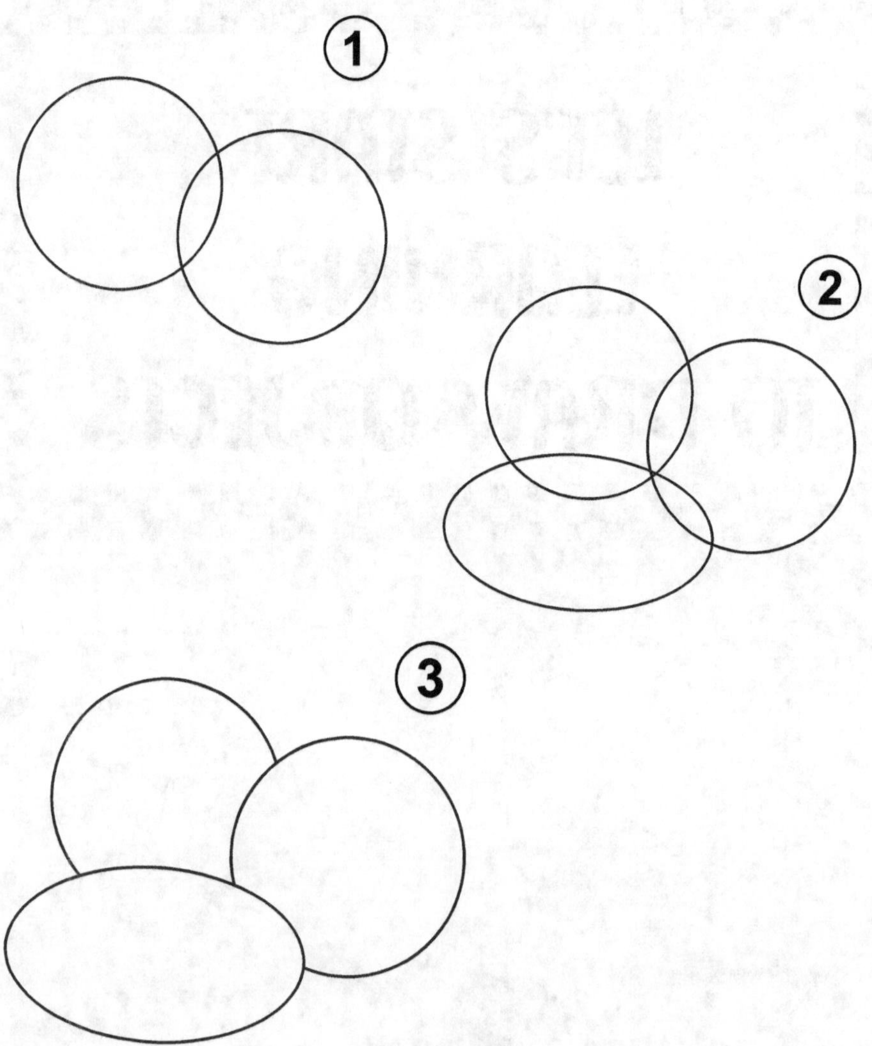

SPORTS BALLS

SECOND STEP

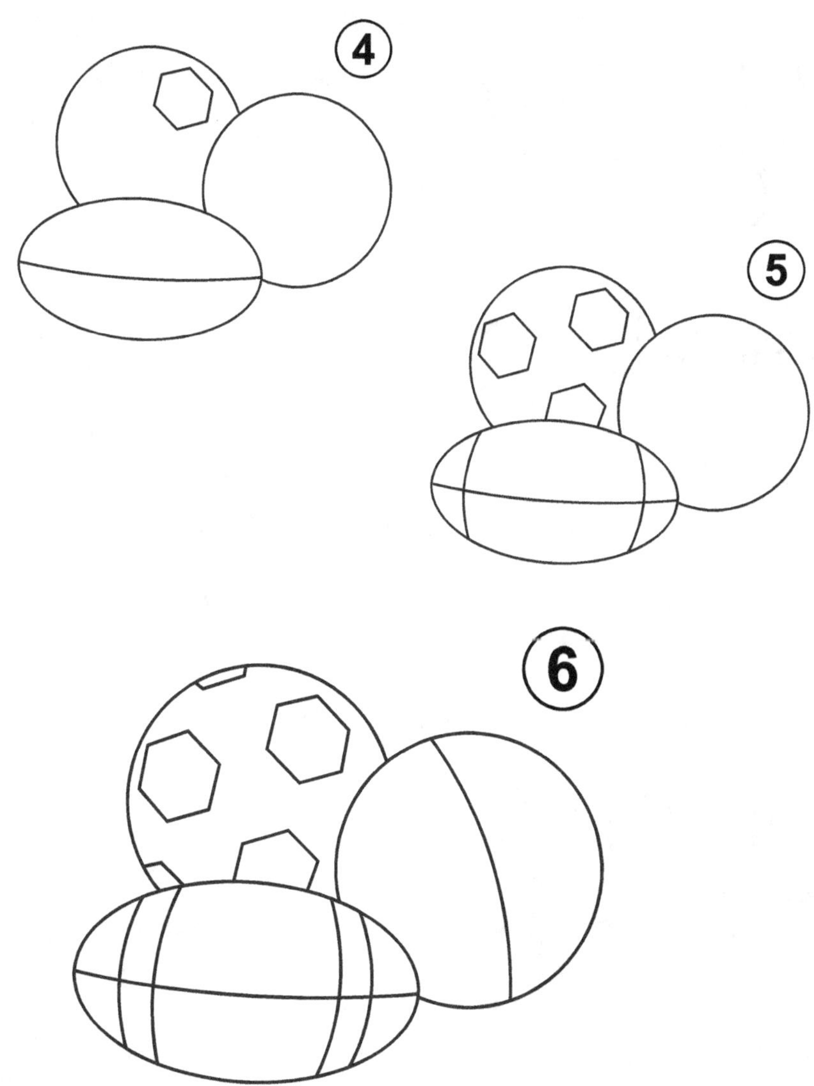

SPORTS BALLS

FINISHED

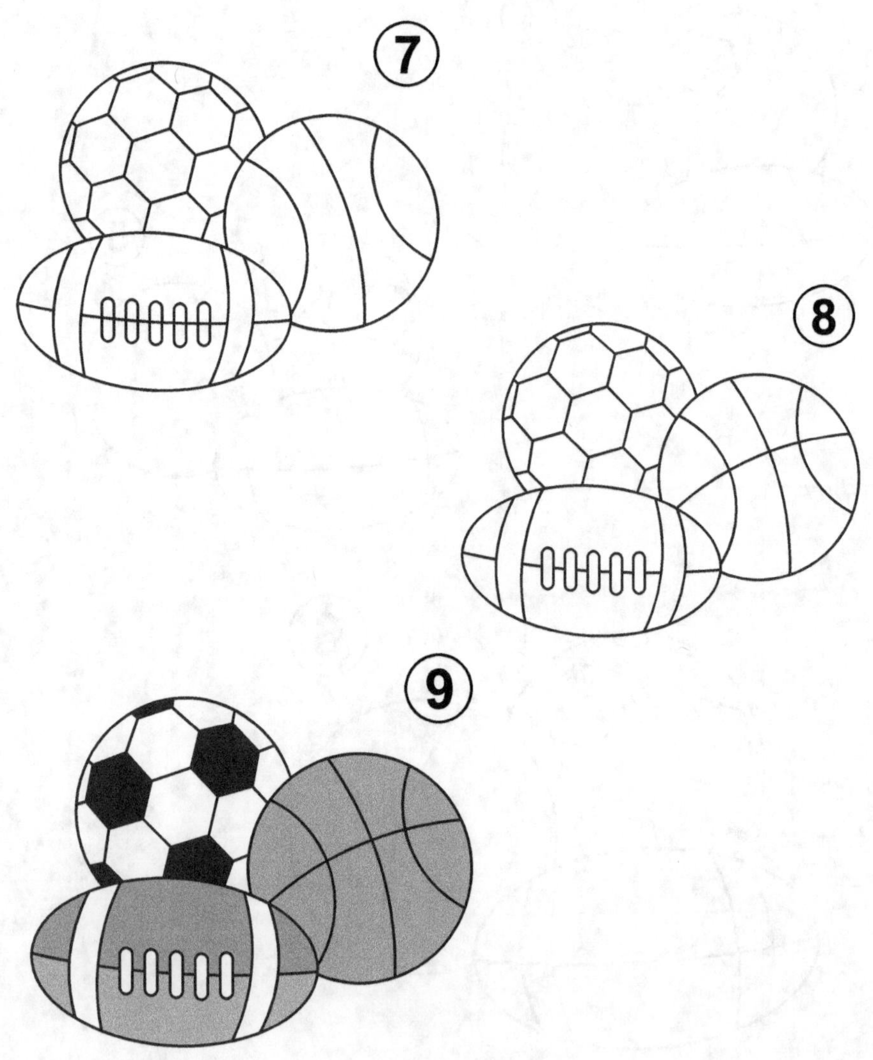

TRY TO DRAW IT HERE

SPORTS BALLS

FIRST STEPS

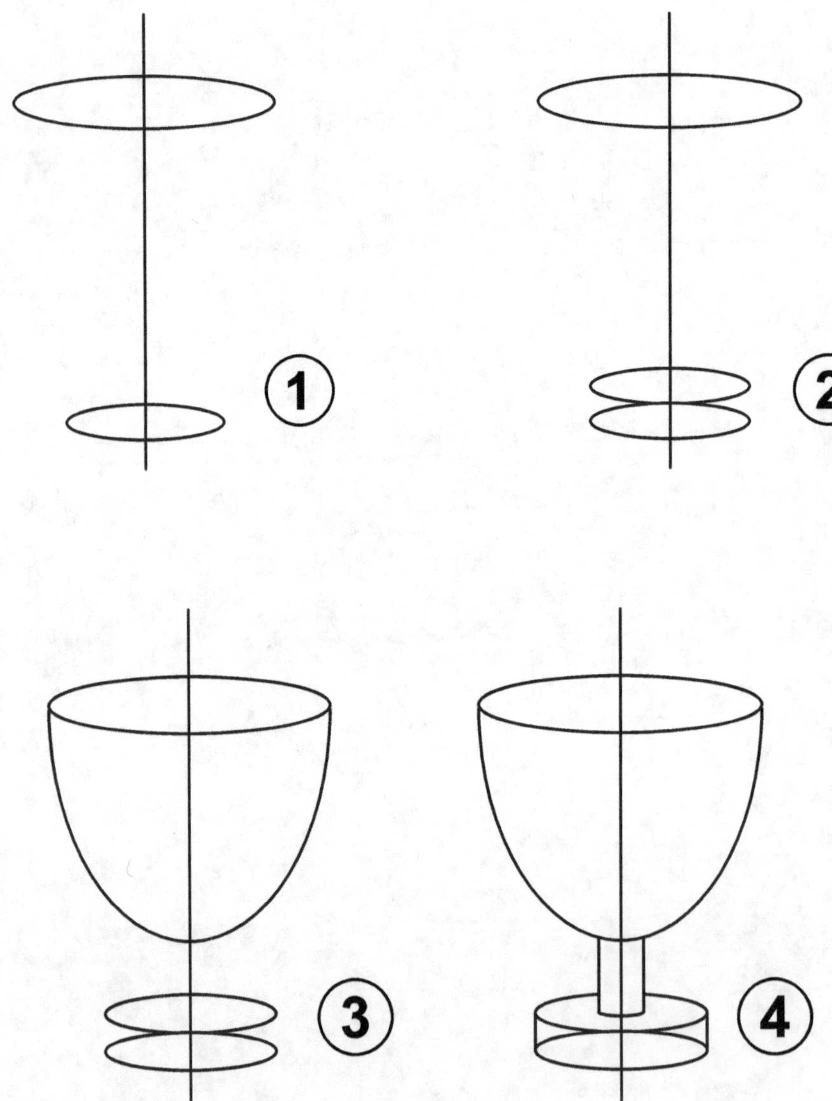

CUP

SECOND STEP

CUP

FINISHED

TRY TO DRAW IT HERE

CUP

BELL

FIRST STEPS

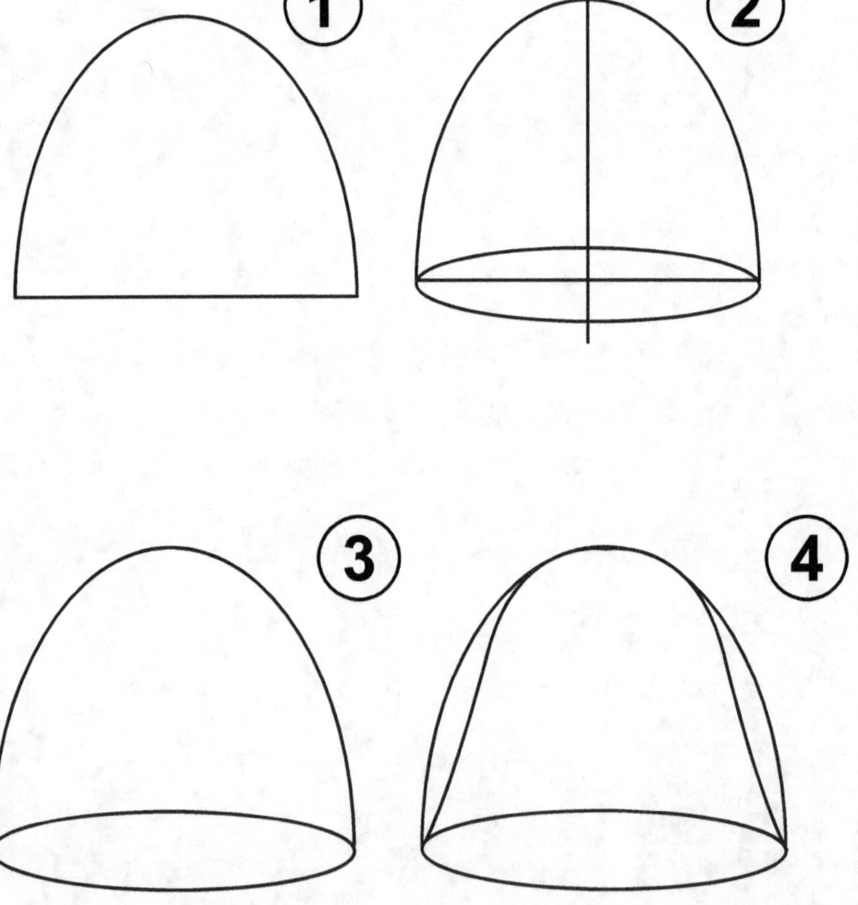

BELL

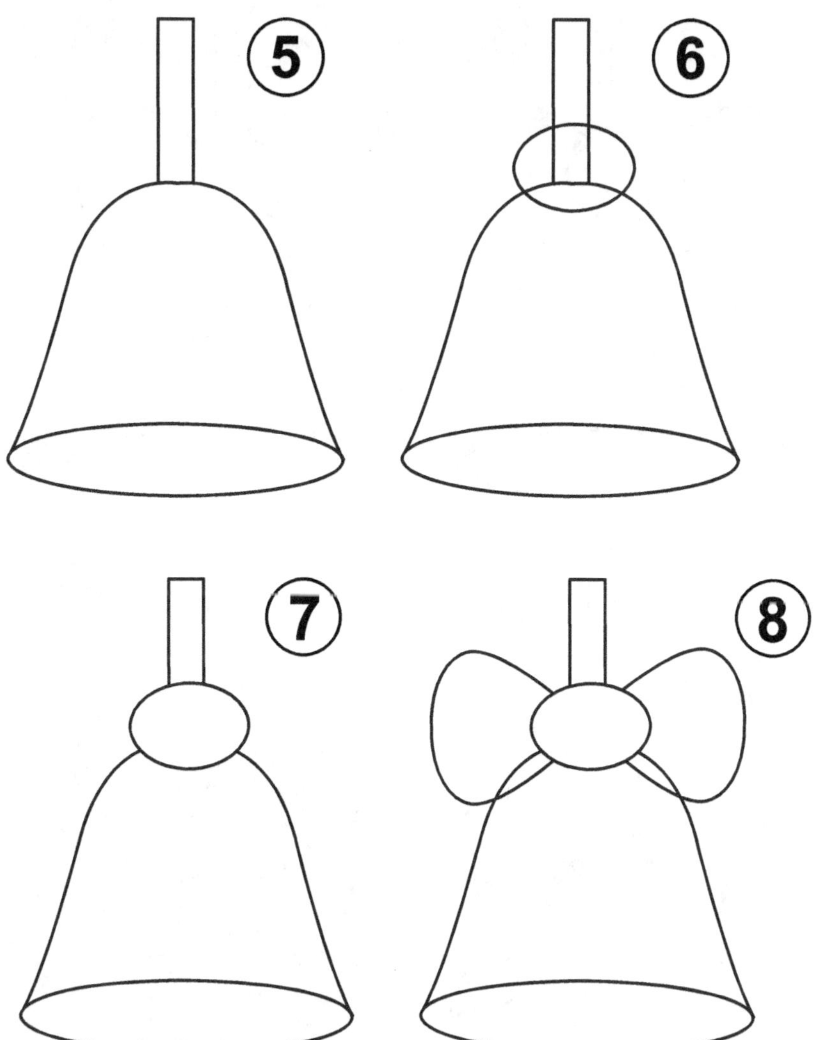

BELL

FINISHED

TRY TO DRAW IT HERE

BELL

HOME

FIRST STEPS

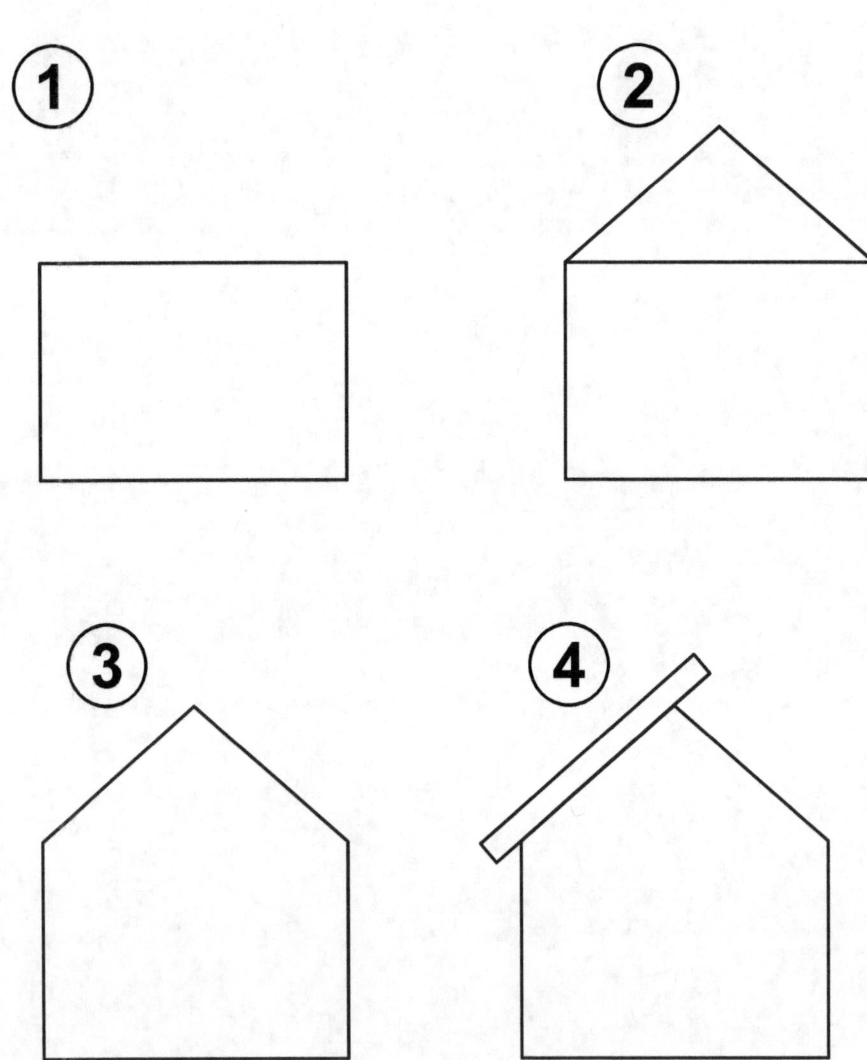

HOME

SECOND STEP

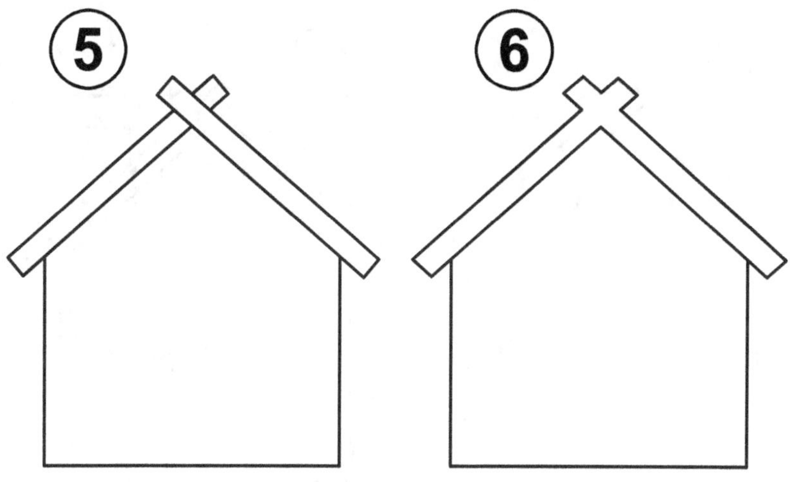

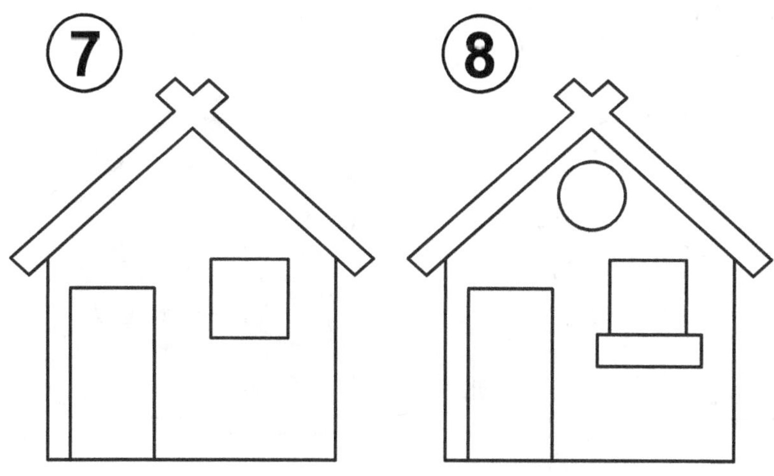

HOME

FINISHED

TRY TO DRAW IT HERE

HOME

FLOWER

FIRST STEPS

FLOWER

SECOND STEP

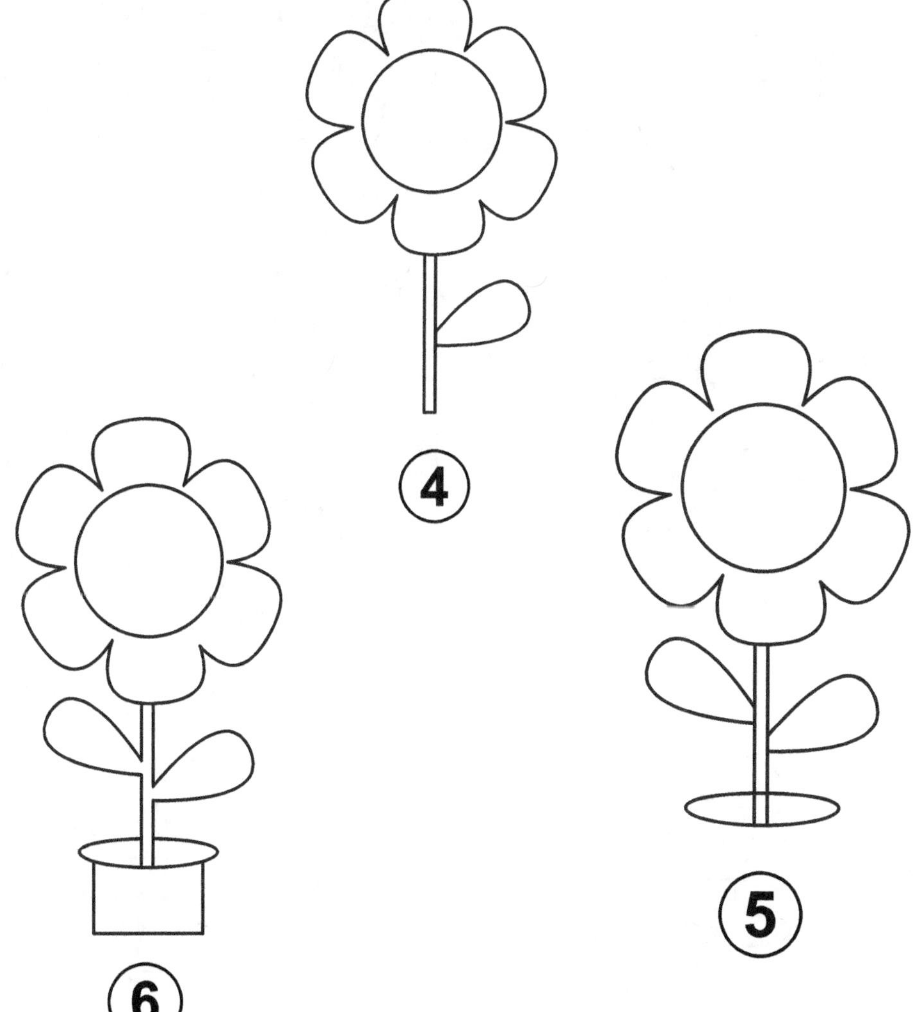

FLOWER

FINISHED

TRY TO DRAW IT HERE

FLOWER

FIRST STEPS

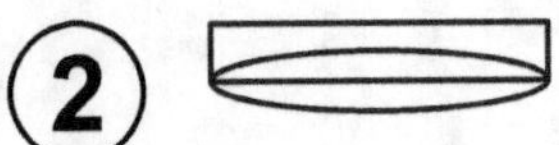

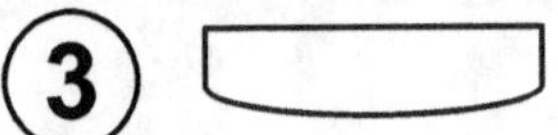

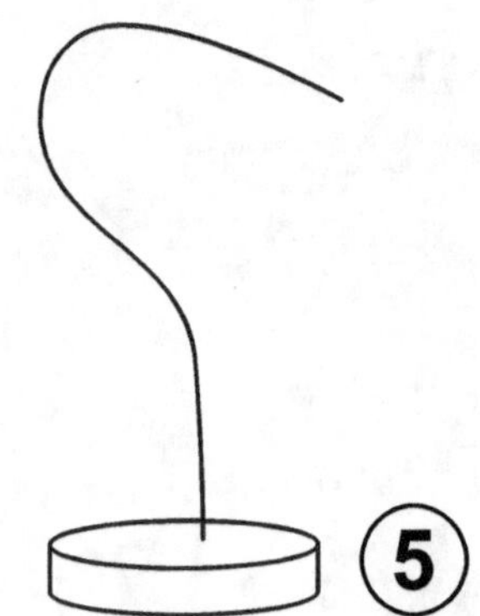

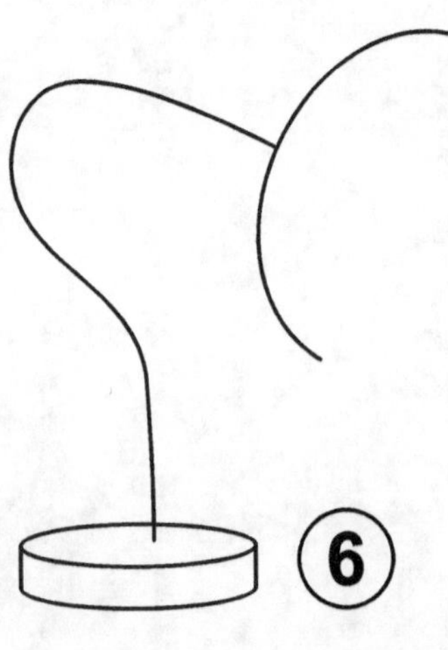

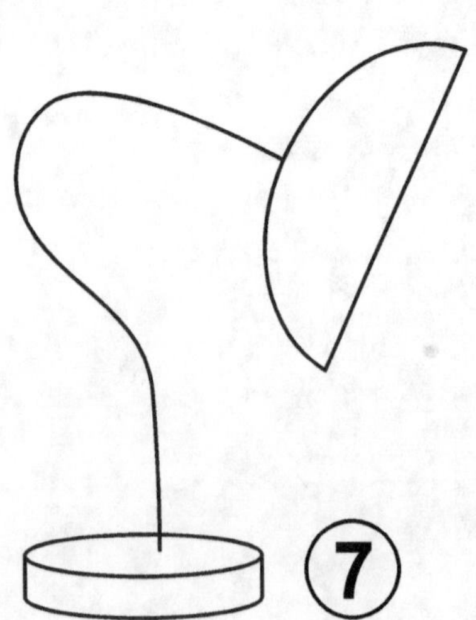

LAMP

SECOND STEP

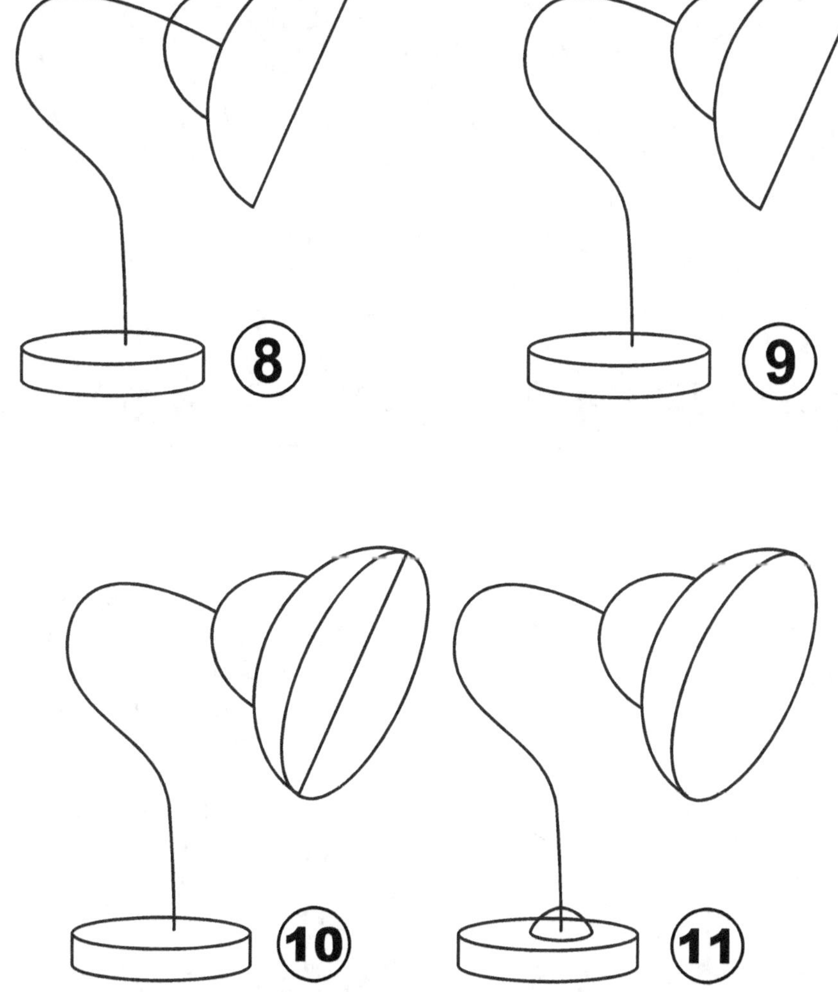

LAMP

FINISHED

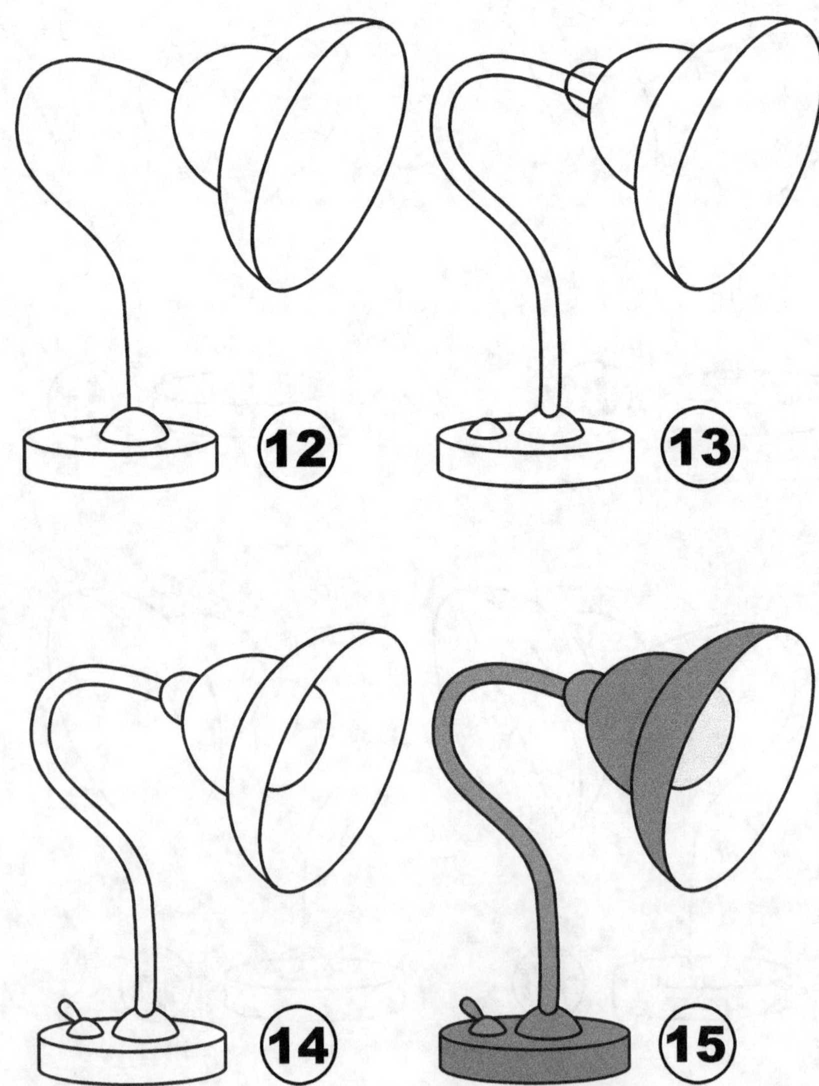

TRY TO DRAW IT HERE

LAMP

CALCULATOR

FIRST STEPS

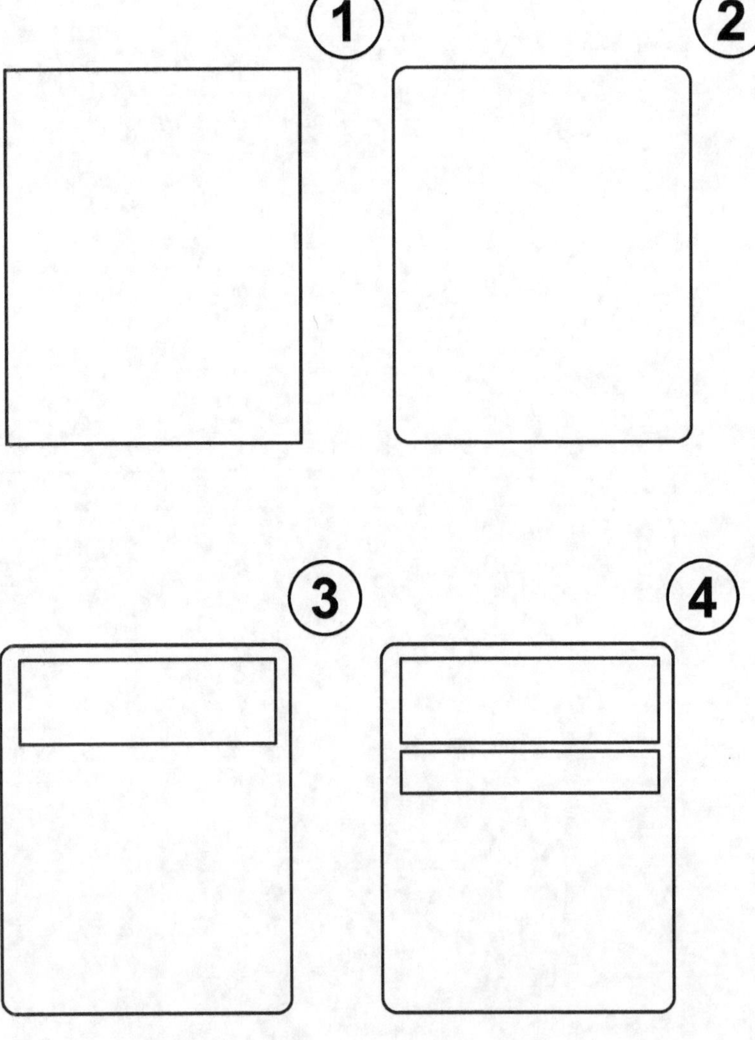

CALCULATOR

SECOND STEP

CALCULATOR

FINISHED

TRY TO DRAW IT HERE

CALCULATOR

BICYCLE

FIRST STEPS

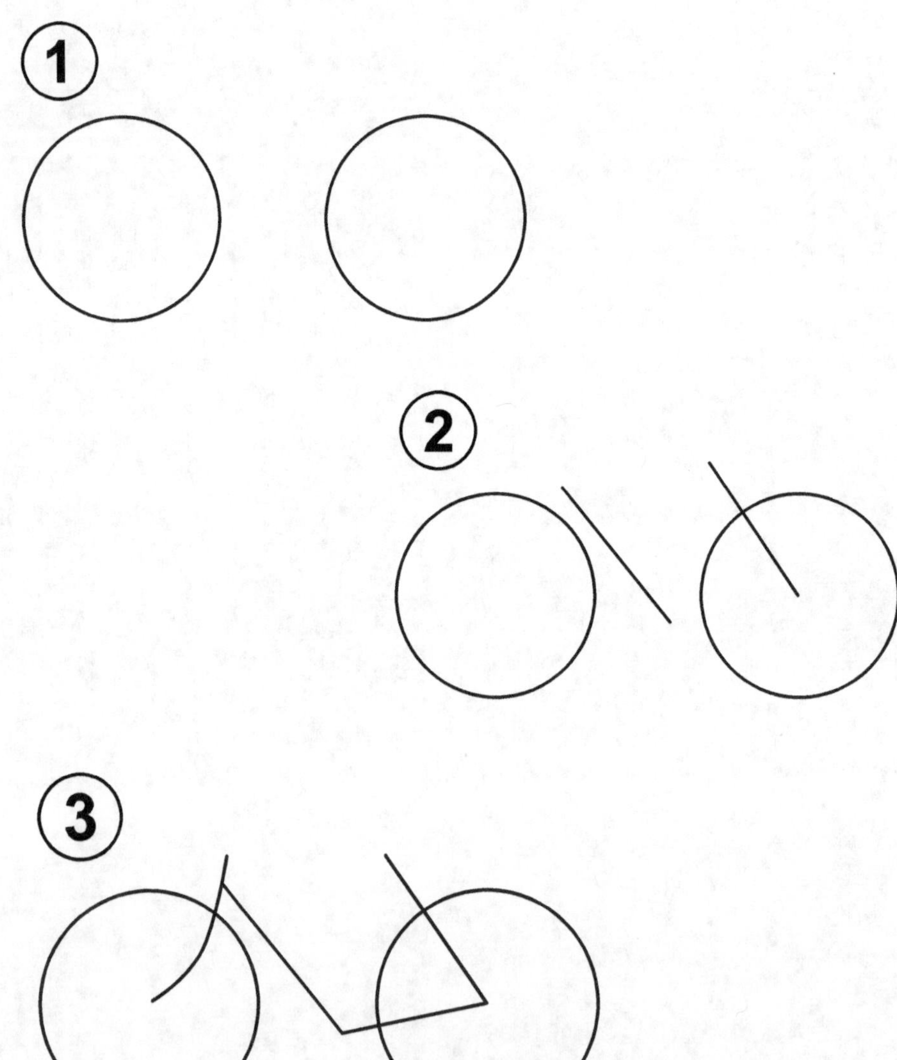

BICYCLE

SECOND STEP

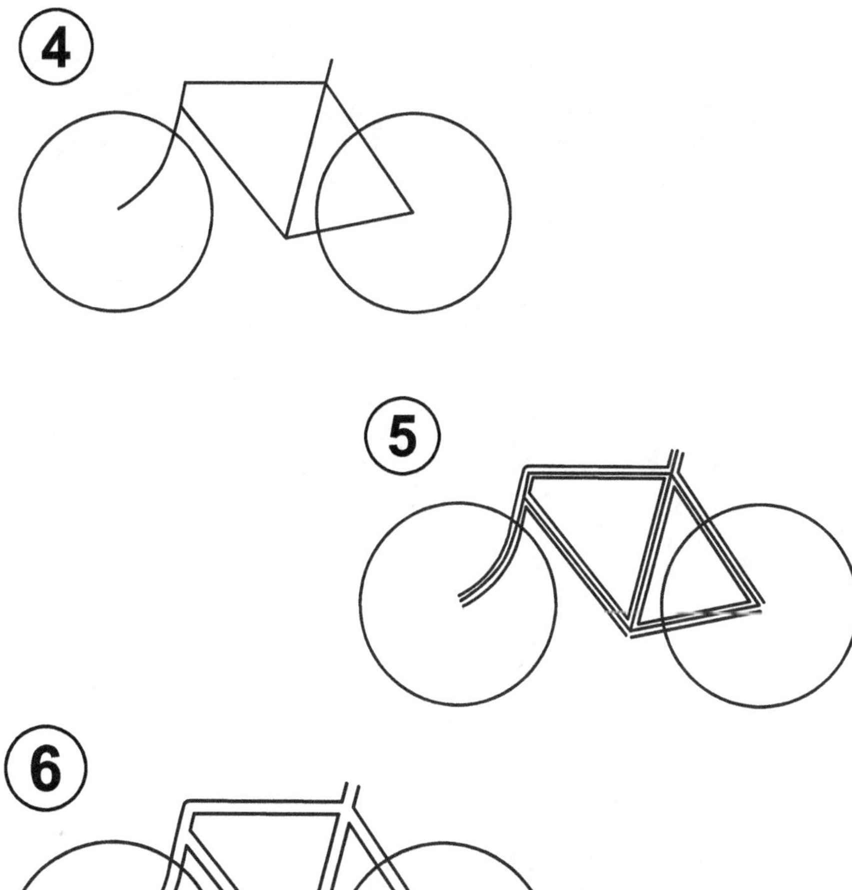

SECOND STEP

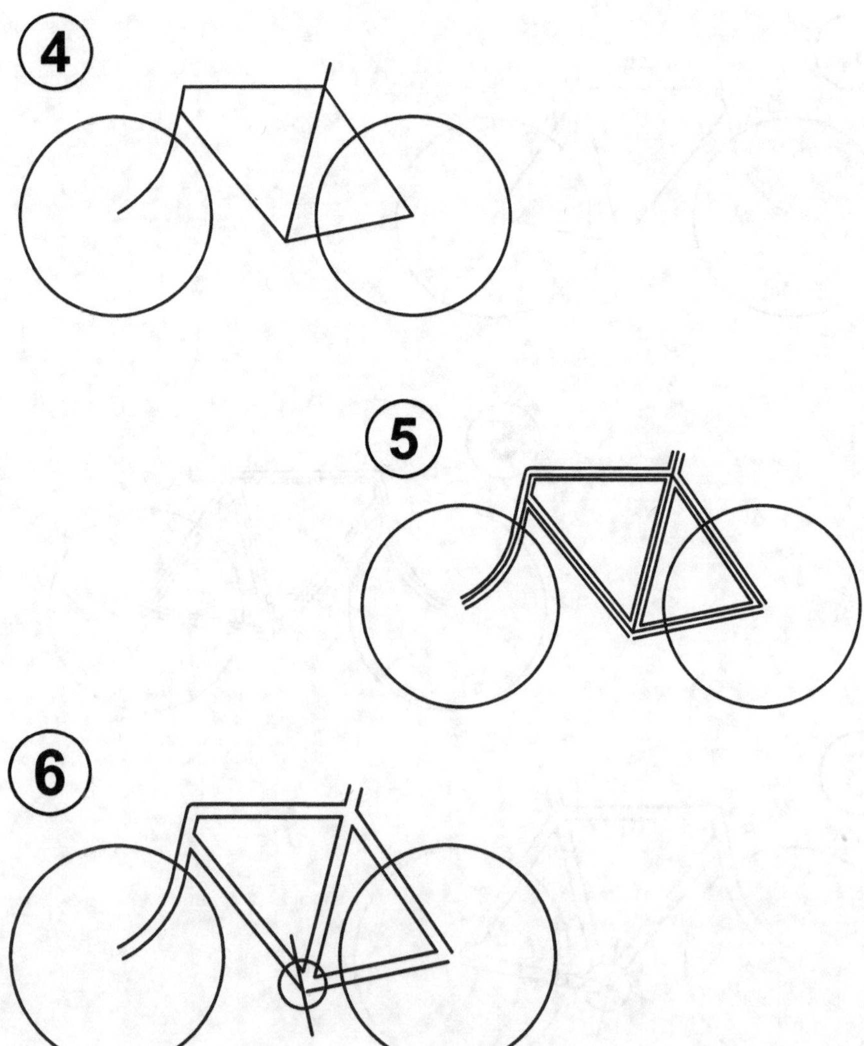

BICYCLE

THIRD STEP

BICYCLE

FINISHED

TRY TO DRAW IT HERE

BICYCLE

CONGRATULATIONS,
YOU ARE NOW
A TRUE ARTIST